Streamflow, Water Quality, and Constituent Loads and Yields, Scituate Reservoir Drainage Area, Rhode Island, Water Year 2011

By Kirk P. Smith

Prepared in cooperation with the Providence Water Supply Board

Open-File Report 2013–1127

U.S. Department of the Interior
U.S. Geological Survey

U.S. Department of the Interior
SALLY JEWELL, Secretary

U.S. Geological Survey
Suzette M. Kimball, Acting Director

U.S. Geological Survey, Reston, Virginia: 2013

For more information on the USGS—the Federal source for science about the Earth, its natural and living resources, natural hazards, and the environment, visit http://www.usgs.gov or call 1–888–ASK–USGS.

For an overview of USGS information products, including maps, imagery, and publications, visit http://www.usgs.gov/pubprod

To order this and other USGS information products, visit http://store.usgs.gov

Suggested citation:
Smith, K.P., 2013, Streamflow, water quality, and constituent loads and yields, Scituate Reservoir drainage area, Rhode Island, water year 2011: U.S. Geological Survey Open-File Report 2013–1127, 32 p., http://pubs.usgs.gov/of/2013/1127/.

Contents

Figures

Tables

Conversion Factors and Datum

Multiply	By	To obtain
Area		
square mile (mi²)	2.590	square kilometer (km²)
Flow rate		
cubic foot per second (ft³/s)	0.02832	cubic meter per second (m³/s)
Mass		
ton, short (2,000 lb)	907.2	kilogram (kg)

Vertical coordinate information is referenced to the North American Vertical Datum of 1988 (NAVD 88).

Horizontal coordinate information is referenced to North American Datum of 1983 (NAD 83).

Concentrations of chemical constituents in water are given either in milligrams per liter (mg/L) or colony forming units per 100 milliliters (CFU/100mL).

Loads of chemical constituents in water are given either in grams or kilograms (or millions of colony forming units for bacteria) per day, month, or year, and yields are given in grams or kilograms (or millions of colony forming units for bacteria) per day, month, or year per square mile.

Abbreviations

CFU	colony forming units
E. coli	*Escherichia coli*
MOVE.1	Maintenance of Variance Extension type 1
NWIS	National Water Inventory System
NTU	nephelometric turbidity units
PCU	platinum cobalt units
PWSB	Providence Water Supply Board
RIDEM	Rhode Island Department of Environmental Management
USGS	U.S. Geological Survey
WY	water year

Streamflow, Water Quality, and Constituent Loads and Yields, Scituate Reservoir Drainage Area, Rhode Island, Water Year 2011

By Kirk P. Smith

Abstract

Streamflow and concentrations of sodium and chloride estimated from records of specific conductance were used to calculate loads of sodium and chloride during water year (WY) 2011 (October 1, 2010, to September 30, 2011), for tributaries to the Scituate Reservoir, Rhode Island. Streamflow and water-quality data used in the study were collected by the U.S. Geological Survey (USGS) or the Providence Water Supply Board (PWSB). Streamflow was measured or estimated by the USGS following standard methods at 23 streamgages; 14 of these streamgages were also equipped with instrumentation capable of continuously monitoring water level, specific conductance, and water temperature. Water-quality samples also were collected at 37 sampling stations by the PWSB and at 14 continuous-record streamgages by the USGS during WY 2011 as part of a long-term sampling program; all stations were in the Scituate Reservoir drainage area. Water-quality data collected by PWSB are summarized by using values of central tendency and are used, in combination with measured (or estimated) streamflows, to calculate loads and yields (loads per unit area) of selected water-quality constituents for WY 2011.

The largest tributary to the reservoir (the Ponaganset River, which was monitored by the USGS) contributed a mean streamflow of about 37 cubic feet per second (ft^3/s) to the reservoir during WY 2011. For the same time period, annual mean[1] streamflows measured (or estimated) for the other monitoring stations in this study ranged from about 0.5 to about 21 ft^3/s. Together, tributaries (equipped with instrumentation capable of continuously monitoring specific conductance) transported about 1,600,000 kg (kilograms) of sodium and 2,600,000 kg of chloride to the Scituate Reservoir during WY 2011; sodium and chloride yields for the tributaries ranged from 9,800 to 53,000 kilograms per square mile (kg/mi^2) and from 15,000 to 90,000 kg/mi^2, respectively.

At the stations where water-quality samples were collected by the PWSB, the median of the median chloride concentrations was 20.0 milligrams per liter (mg/L), median nitrite concentration was 0.002 mg/L as nitrogen (N), median nitrate concentration was 0.01 mg/L as N, median orthophosphate concentration was 0.07 mg/L as phosphorus, and median concentrations of total coliform and *Escherichia coli (E. coli)* bacteria were 33 and 23 colony forming units per 100 milliliters (CFU/100mL), respectively. The medians of the median daily loads (and yields) of chloride, nitrite, nitrate, orthophosphate, and total coliform and *E. coli* bacteria were 230 kilograms per day (kg/d) (80 kilograms per day per square mile (kg/d/mi^2)); 10 grams per day (g/d) (6.3 grams per day per square mile (g/d/mi^2)); 110 g/d (29 g/d/mi^2); 610 g/d (270 g/d/mi^2); 4,600 million colony forming units per day (CFUx10^6/d) (2,500 CFUx10^6/d/mi^2); and 1,800 CFUx10^6/d (810 CFUx10^6/d/mi^2), respectively.

---

[1] The arithmetic mean of the individual daily mean discharges for the year noted or for the designated period.

Introduction

The Scituate Reservoir is the primary source of drinking water for more than 60 percent of the population of Rhode Island (R.I.). It covers about 94 square miles (mi^2) in parts of the towns of Cranston, Foster, Glocester, Johnston, and Scituate, R.I. (fig. 1). Information about the water quality of the reservoir and its tributaries is important for management of the water supply and for the protection of human health. The Providence Water Supply Board (PWSB), the agency responsible for the management and distribution of the Scituate Reservoir water supply, has been monitoring and assessing water quality in the reservoir and reservoir drainage area for more than 60 years.

Since 1993, the U.S. Geological Survey (USGS) has been cooperating with the PWSB and the Rhode Island Department of Environmental Management (RIDEM) to measure streamflow in tributaries to the Scituate Reservoir. Since 2009, streamflow has been continuously measured at 14 streamgages in the drainage area and periodically measured at 9 additional streamgages on tributaries in the drainage area. At these 9 partial-record streamgages, daily mean streamflow has been estimated by using methods developed by the USGS (Hirsch, 1982). The USGS also has been continuously measuring specific conductance at 14 monitoring stations since 2009. Equations that relate specific conductance to concentrations of sodium and chloride in streamwater were developed as part of a previous USGS/ PWSB cooperative study (Nimiroski and Waldron, 2002). These equations, updated here and used together with measured (or estimated) streamflows, allow for nearly continuous estimation of sodium and chloride loads to the reservoir.

Currently (2011), the PWSB regularly collects water-quality samples from 37 tributaries, either monthly or quarterly. Water-quality results are summarized by station number and constituent or parameter in annual reports published by the PWSB. In addition, the USGS has published reports that have compiled and tabulated streamflow (measured or estimated by the USGS) and water-quality data (collected by the PWSB) (Breault and others, 2000; Nimiroski and others, 2008; Breault, 2010; Breault and Campbell, 2010a,b,c,d; Breault and Smith, 2010; Smith and Breault, 2011).

This report presents data on streamflow, water quality, and loads and yields of selected constituents for water year (WY) 2011[2] in the Scituate Reservoir drainage area. These data were collected as parts of studies done by the USGS in cooperation with the PWSB and the RIDEM. A summary of measured and estimated streamflows is presented for the 14 continuous-record and 9 partial-record streamgages in the drainage area. Estimated monthly and annual loads (and yields) of sodium and chloride are presented for the 14 streamgages at which specific conductance is continuously monitored by the USGS. Summary statistics for water-quality

data collected by the PWSB for 37 sampling stations during WY 2011 also are presented, and these data were used to calculate loads and yields of selected water-quality constituents (table 1).

Streamflow Data Collection and Estimation

Streamflow and water-quality data were collected by the USGS or the PWSB (table 1). Streamflow was measured or estimated by the USGS at 23 streamgages. Measured and estimated streamflows are necessary to estimate water volume and water-quality constituent loads and yields from tributary basins. Stream stage is measured every 10 minutes at most continuous-record streamgages. Streamflow is computed with a stage-discharge relation (or rating), which is developed on the basis of periodic manual measurements of streamflow. Daily mean streamflow at a streamgage is calculated by dividing the total volume of water that passes the streamgage each day by 86,400, the number of seconds in a day. Periodic manual streamflow measurements at partial-record streamgages are used with concurrent continuous-record measurements from streamgages in hydrologically similar drainage areas to estimate a continuous record at the partial-record streamgage. Specifically, continuous streamflow records for the nine partial-record sites in the Scituate Reservoir drainage area were estimated by using the Maintenance of Variance Extension type 1 (MOVE.1) method, as described by Ries and Friesz (2000); data needed to estimate streamflows at partial-record sites were retrieved from the USGS National Water Inventory System (NWIS; http://waterdata.usgs.gov/nwis/). The upper and lower 90-percent confidence limits about the estimated mean annual streamflows, as described by Tasker and Driver (1988), also are presented in table 2. These data indicate that there is a 90-percent chance that the estimated mean annual streamflow is somewhere between the upper and lower 90-percent confidence limits.

Continuous-record streamgages were operated and maintained by the USGS during WY 2011 in cooperation with RIDEM (USGS streamgage01115098) and the PWSB (fig. 1, table 1). Streamflow data for these streamgages wee collected at 10 or 15-minute intervals (near-real-time streamflow data), were updated at 1-hour intervals on the World Wide Web (WWW), and are available through the NWIS Web Interface (NWIS Web; U.S. Geological Survey, 2007). Error associated with measured streamflows was generally within about 15 percent (U.S. Geological Survey, unpublished data); upper and lower 90-percent confidence limits calculated by methods described by the National Institute of Standards and Technology/SEmiconductor MAnufacturing TECHnology (2003) are shown in table 2.

---

[2] October 1, 2010, to September 30, 2011.

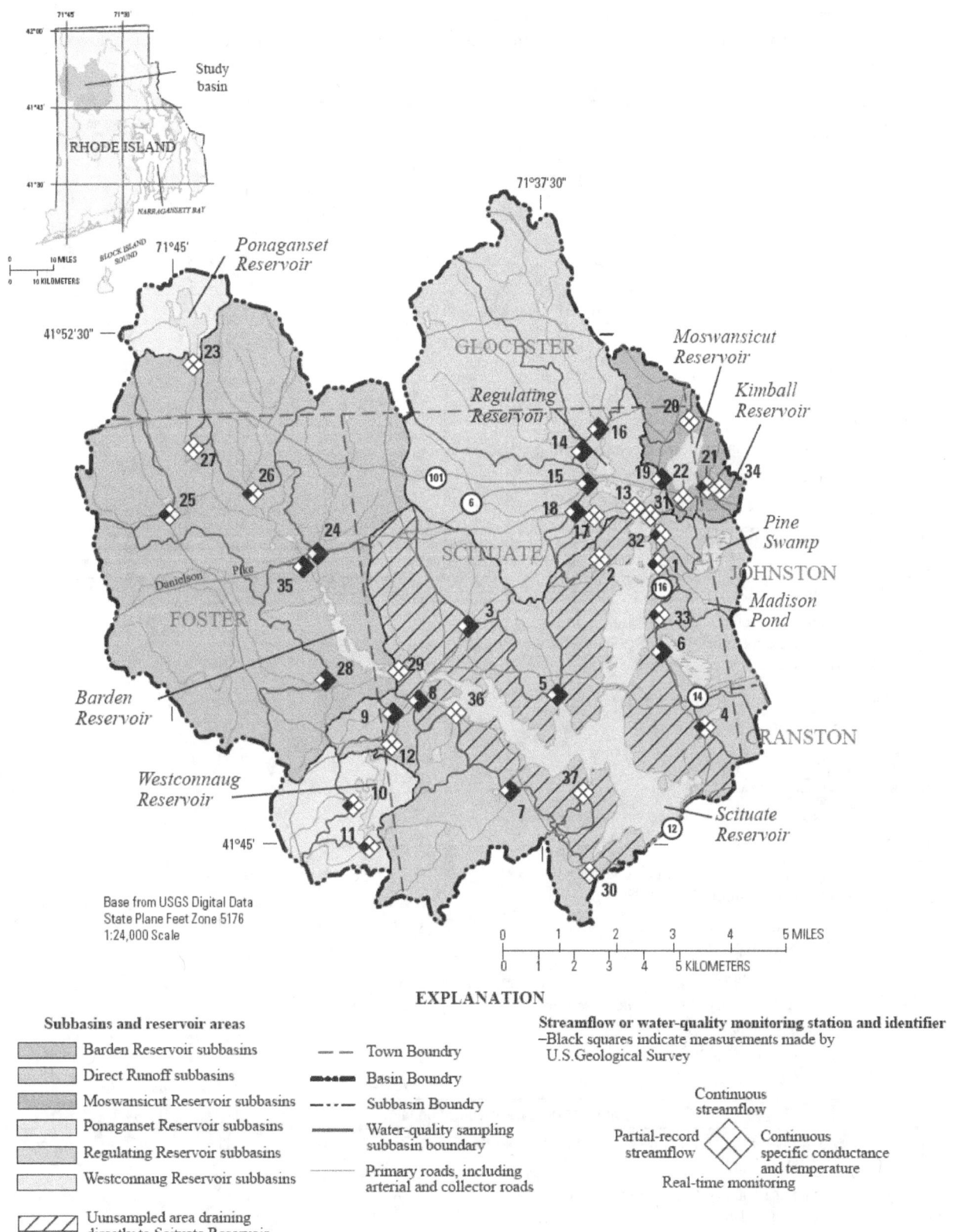

Figure 1. Locations of tributary-reservoir subbasins and streamgage and water-quality monitoring stations in the Scituate Reservoir drainage area, Rhode Island.

Table 1.   Providence Water Supply Board water-quality sampling stations, water-quality samples, and available streamflow and continuous monitoring stations by tributary reservoir subbasin, in the Scituate Reservoir drainage area, Rhode Island, October 1, 2010, to September 30, 2011.

[PWSB, Providence Water Supply Board; USGS, U.S. Geological Survey; no., number; mi², square miles; QW, water quality; M, monthly; Q, quarterly; Y, yes; N, no; Na, sodium; Cl, chloride; --, none; alternate station names given in parenthesis for stations where different historical names were used for the same sampling location by Providence Water]

PWSB station no.	USGS station no.	Station name	Drainage area (mi²)	Frequency of QW sample collection	Number of samples collected by Providence Water[1]	Daily estimated Na and Cl loads	Estimated stream-flow cal-culated
		Barden Reservior Subbasin					
24	01115190	Dolly Cole Brook	4.90	M	10	Y	N
25	01115200	Shippee Brook	2.35	Q	3	N	Y
26	01115185	Windsor Brook	4.32	Q	4	N	Y
27	011151845	Unnamed Tributary to Ponaganset River (Unnamed Brook B, Unnamed Brook West of Windsor Brook)	0.10	Q	2	N	N
28	01115265	Barden Reservoir (Hemlock Brook)	8.72	M	12	Y	N
29	01115271	Ponaganset River (Barden Stream)	33.0	M	12	N	N
35	01115187	Ponaganset River	14.0	M	11	Y	N
		Direct Runoff Subbasin					
1	01115180	Brandy Brook	1.57	M	11	N	Y
2	01115181	Unnamed Tributary 2 to Scituate Reservoir (Unnamed Brook North of Bullhead Brook)	0.15	Q	1	N	N
3	01115280	Cork Brook	1.79	M	11	Y	N
4	01115400	Kent Brook (Betty Pond Stream)	0.85	M	11	N	Y
5	01115184	Spruce Brook	1.22	Q	3	Y	N
6	01115183	Quonapaug Brook	1.96	M	11	Y	N
7	01115297	Wilbur Hollow Brook	4.32	M	10	Y	N
8	01115276	Westconnaug Brook (Westconnaug Reservoir)	5.18	M	9	Y	N
9	01115275	Bear Tree Brook	0.62	Q	2	Y	N
30	01115350	Unnamed Tributary 4 to Scituate Reservoir (Coventry Brook, Knight Brook)	0.78	Q	2	N	N
31	01115177	Toad Pond	0.04	Q	1	N	N
32	01115178	Unnamed Tributary 1 to Scituate Reservoir (Pine Swamp Brook)	0.45	Q	3	N	Y
33	01115182	Unnamed Tributary 3 to Scituate Reservoir (Hall's Estate Brook)	0.28	Q	4	N	Y
36	--	Outflow from King Pond	0.77	Q	3	N	N
37	--	Fire Tower Stream	0.15	Q	2	N	N
		Moswansicut Reservoir Subbasin					
19	01115170	Moswansicut Reservoir (Moswansicut Stream North, Moswansicut Pond)	3.25	M	11	Y	N
20	01115160	Unnamed Tributary 1 to Moswansicut Reservoir (Blanchard Brook)	1.18	M	10	N	N
21	01115165	Unnamed Tributary 2 to Moswansicut Reservoir (Brook from Kimball Reservoir)	0.29	Q	2	N	Y
22	01115167	Moswansicut Reservoir (Moswansicut Stream South)	0.22	M	9	N	N
34	01115164	Kimball Stream	0.27	Q	1	N	N

Table 1. Providence Water Supply Board water-quality sampling stations, water-quality samples, and available streamflow and continuous monitoring stations by tributary reservoir subbasin, in the Scituate Reservoir drainage area, Rhode Island, October 1, 2010, to September 30, 2011.—Continued

[PWSB, Providence Water Supply Board; USGS, U.S. Geological Survey; no., number; mi², square miles; QW, water quality; M, monthly; Q, quarterly; Y, yes; N, no; Na, sodium; Cl, chloride; --, none; alternate station names given in parenthesis for stations where different historical names were used for the same sampling location by Providence Water]

PWSB station no.	USGS station no.	Station name	Drainage area (mi²)	Frequency of QW sample collection	Number of samples collected by Providence Water[1]	Daily estimated Na and Cl loads	Estimated stream-flow cal-culated
Ponaganset Reservoir Subbasin
23	011151843	Ponaganset Reservoir	1.92	M	12	N	N
Regulating Reservoir Subbasin
13	01115176	Regulating Reservoir	22.1	M	11	N	N
14	01115110	Huntinghouse Brook	6.23	M	10	Y	N
15	01115114	Rush Brook	4.70	M	11	Y	N
16	01115098	Peeptoad Brook (Harrisdale Brook)	4.96	M	11	Y	N
17	01115119	Dexter Pond (Paine Pond)	0.22	Q	2	N	N
18	01115120	Unnamed Tributary to Regulating Reservoir (Unnamed Brook A)	0.28	Q	1	Y	N
Westconnaug Reservoir Subbasin
10	01115274	Westconnaug Brook	1.48	M	10	N	Y
11	01115273	Unnamed Tributary to Westconnaug Reservoir (Unnamed Brook south of Westconnaug Reservoir)	0.72	Q	2	N	Y
12	011152745	Unnamed Tributary to Westconnaug Brook (Unnamed Brook north of Westconnaug Reservoir)	0.16	Q	1	N	N

[1]Not all samples were analyzed for all water-quality properties or constituents.

Table 2.   Measured or estimated annual mean streamflow for tributary streams in the Scituate Reservoir drainage area, Rhode Island, October 1, 2010, through September 30, 2011.

[PWSB, Providence Water Supply Board; USGS, U.S. Geological Survey; no., number; ft³/s, cubic feet per second; ft³/s/mi², cubic feet per second per square mile; alternate station names given in parenthesis for stations where different historical names were used for the same sampling location by the Providence Water Supply Board]

PWSB station no.	USGS station no.	Station name	Annual mean streamflow (ft³/s)	Upper 90-percent confidence interval (ft³/s)	Lower 90-percent confidence interval (ft³/s)	Annual mean streamflow (ft³/s/mi²)
		Barden Reservoir Subbasin				
24	01115190	Dolly Cole Brook	11	13	10	2.3
25	01115200	Shippee Brook	5.8	20	1.6	2.5
26	01115185	Windsor Brook	8.8	36	2.2	2.0
28	01115265	Barden Reservoir (Hemlock Brook)	21	24	19	2.4
35	01115187	Ponaganset River	37	41	34	2.7
		Direct Runoff Subbasin				
1	01115180	Brandy Brook	2.5	4.6	1.4	1.6
3	01115280	Cork Brook	3.4	3.9	2.9	1.9
4	01115400	Kent Brook (Betty Pond Stream)	2.5	12	0.52	2.9
5	01115184	Spruce Brook	2.3	2.4	2.1	1.9
6	01115183	Quonapaug Brook	4.0	4.4	3.7	2.1
7	01115297	Wilbur Hollow Brook	8.2	8.9	7.5	1.9
8	01115276	Westconnaug Brook (Westconnaug Reservoir)	7.5	7.8	7.1	1.4
9	01115275	Bear Tree Brook	1.4	1.5	1.3	2.2
32	01115178	Unnamed Tributary 1 to Scituate Reservoir (Pine Swamp Brook)	0.64	1.3	0.32	1.4
33	01115182	Unnamed Tributary 3 to Scituate Reservoir (Hall's Estate Brook)	0.59	1.6	0.21	2.1
		Moswansicut Reservoir Subbasin				
19	01115170	Moswansicut Reservoir (Moswansicut Stream North, Moswansicut Pond)	6.3	6.7	5.8	1.9
21	01115165	Unnamed Tributary 2 to Moswansicut Reservoir (Blanchard Brook)	0.69	1.5	0.31	2.4
		Regulating Reservoir Subbasin				
14	01115110	Huntinghouse Brook	13	15	11	2.2
15	01115115	Rush Brook	9.7	11	8.3	2.1
16	01115098	Peeptoad Brook (Harrisdale Brook)	11	13	9.7	2.3
18	01115120	Unnamed Tributary to Regulating Reservoir (Unnamed Brook A)	0.51	0.59	0.43	1.8
		Westconnaug Reservoir Subbasin				
10	01115274	Westconnaug Brook	2.4	4.2	1.3	1.6
11	01115273	Unnamed Tributary to Westconnaug Reservoir (Unnamed Brook South of Westconnaug Reservoir)	1.3	2.3	0.79	1.9

Water-Quality Data Collection and Analysis

Water-quality data were collected by the USGS or PWSB. Concentrations of sodium and chloride were estimated (by the USGS) from continuous or partial records of specific conductance from 14 of the 23 streamgages. Water-quality samples were collected monthly or quarterly at 37 sampling stations in the Scituate Reservoir drainage area by the PWSB during WY 2011 as part of a long-term sampling program. Daily loads of bacteria, chloride, nitrite, nitrate, and orthophosphate were calculated for 23 streamgages where streamflow data were collected by the USGS, and water-quality samples were collected by the PWSB. Yields were calculated by dividing load by drainage area.

Data Collected by the U.S. Geological Survey

Water quality was monitored in a periodic water-quality sampling program that included measurements by automatic specific-conductance probes. The USGS collected and analyzed the specific conductance data. Specific conductance was measured by the USGS at 10- or 15-minute intervals at the 14 continuous-record streamgages (fig. 1). Measurements were made by using an instream probe and standard USGS methods for continuous streamwater-quality monitoring (Wagner and others, 2006).

Concentrations of sodium and chloride were estimated from continuous or periodic measurements of specific conductance by using equations that were developed by the USGS to relate specific conductance to concentrations of sodium and chloride (equations 1 and 2). These regression equations were developed by the MOVE.1 method (also known as the line of organic correlation; Helsel and Hirsch, 1992) on the basis of concurrent measurements of specific conductance along with sodium and chloride concentrations measured in water-quality samples collected by the USGS from tributaries in the Scituate Reservoir drainage area (U.S. Geological Survey, 2001):

$$C_{Cl} = \left(Spc^{m} \right) \times b , \tag{1}$$

$$C_{Na} = \left(Spc^{m} \right) \times b , \tag{2}$$

where

C_{Cl}	is the chloride concentration, in milligrams per liter (mg/L);
C_{Na}	is the sodium concentration, in mg/L; and
Spc	is the specific conductance, in microsiemens per centimeter at 25° Celsius;
m	is the slope from the MOVE.1 analysis (table 3); and
b	is the intercept from the MOVE.1 analysis (table 3).

MOVE.1 was chosen for regression analysis to maintain variance (Hirsch and Gilroy, 1984). Some missing values of specific conductance were estimated. In these cases, values of specific conductance were estimated by proportional distribution between recorded values.

Data Collected by the Providence Water Supply Board

Water-quality samples were collected at fixed stations on 37 tributaries by the PWSB. Sampling was done monthly at 19 stations and quarterly at another 18 stations (table 1) during WY 2011. Water-quality samples were not collected during specific weather conditions; rather, a strictly periodic water-quality sampling schedule was followed so that water-quality samples would be representative of various weather conditions. However, sometimes samples could not be collected because tributaries at the sampling stations were dry or frozen. When possible, water-quality samples were collected by dipping the sample bottle into the tributary at the center of flow (Richard Blodgett, PWSB, written commun., 2005). Samples were transported on ice to the PWSB water-quality laboratory at the P.J. Holton Water Purification Plant in Scituate, R.I. Water-quality properties and constituent concentrations were measured by using unfiltered water samples. These water-quality properties included pH, temperature, acidity, alkalinity, color, turbidity, and concentrations of chloride, nitrite, nitrate, orthophosphate, and bacteria (*Escherichia coli (E. coli)* and total coliform). More information on sample-collection, analytical, and quality-control procedures can be found in the Providence Water Supply Board Quality Assurance Program Manual (Providence Water Supply Board Water Quality Laboratory, 2003).

The PWSB collected samples during a wide range of flow conditions. The daily mean flow-duration curve for the Quonapaug Brook at North Scituate (USGS streamgage 01115183) for WY 2011 is shown in figure 2. The curve

Table 3.   Regression equation coefficients used to estimate concentrations of chloride and sodium from values of specific conductance for each U.S. Geological Survey monitoring station in the Scituate Reservoir drainage area, Rhode Island, October 1, 2010, through September 30, 2011.

[PWSB, Providence Water Supply Board; USGS, U.S. Geological Survey; no., number; RMSE, root mean square error]

PWSB station no.	USGS station no.	Chloride			Sodium		
		Slope	Intercept	RMSE	Slope	Intercept	RMSE
24	01115190	0.1334	1.1013	0.030	0.1074	1.0431	0.035
28	01115265	0.1334	1.1013	0.030	0.1074	1.0431	0.035
35	01115187	0.1334	1.1013	0.030	0.1074	1.0431	0.035
3	01115280	0.1334	1.1013	0.030	0.1074	1.0431	0.035
5	01115184	0.0772	1.1901	0.037	0.0760	1.0808	0.037
6	01115183	0.1334	1.1013	0.030	0.1074	1.0431	0.035
7	01115297	0.0772	1.1901	0.037	0.0760	1.0808	0.037
8	01115276	0.1334	1.1013	0.030	0.1074	1.0431	0.035
9	01115275	0.1334	1.1013	0.030	0.1074	1.0431	0.035
19	01115170	0.1334	1.1013	0.030	0.1074	1.0431	0.035
14	01115110	0.0772	1.1901	0.037	0.0760	1.0808	0.037
15	01115114	0.1334	1.1013	0.030	0.1074	1.0431	0.035
16	01115098	0.1334	1.1013	0.030	0.1074	1.0431	0.035
18	01115120	0.1334	1.1013	0.030	0.1074	1.0431	0.035

represents the percentage of time that each flow was exceeded at this station. The flows at this station on days when water-quality samples were collected are represented by the plotted points superimposed on the curve. Samples were collected at flow durations ranging from the 3rd percentile to the 98th percentile; this range indicates that the water-quality samples collected in WY 2011 represented a wide range of flow conditions during that water year.

Estimating Daily, Monthly, and Annual Loads and Yields

Daily, monthly, and annual sodium and chloride loads in kilograms were estimated for all streamgages for which continuous-streamflow and specific-conductance data were available for WY 2011. Daily flow-weighted concentrations of sodium and chloride were calculated by multiplying instantaneous flows by concurrent concentrations of sodium and chloride (estimated from measurements of specific conductance) for each day and dividing by the total flow for that day. Daily sodium and chloride loads were estimated by multiplying daily flow-weighted concentrations of sodium and chloride in milligrams per liter by daily discharge (in liters per day). Daily data was summed to estimate monthly or annual loads.

Daily loads of water-quality constituents (in samples collected by the PWSB) were calculated for all sampling dates during WY 2011 (table 4, at back of report) for which periodic or continuous-streamflow data were available (table 1). These loads were calculated by multiplying constituent concentrations in milligrams or colony forming units (CFU) per liter in single samples by the daily discharge (in liters per day) for the day on which each sample was collected. The flows, which in some cases were estimates, were assumed to be representative of the flow at the time of the sample collection. Loads in grams or kilograms (or millions of CFUs for bacteria) per day and yields in grams or kilograms (or millions of CFUs for bacteria) per day per square mile were calculated for bacteria, chloride, nitrite, nitrate, and orthophosphate from this water-quality data. Censored data (or concentrations reported as less than method detection limits) were replaced with concentrations equal to one-half the method detection limit.

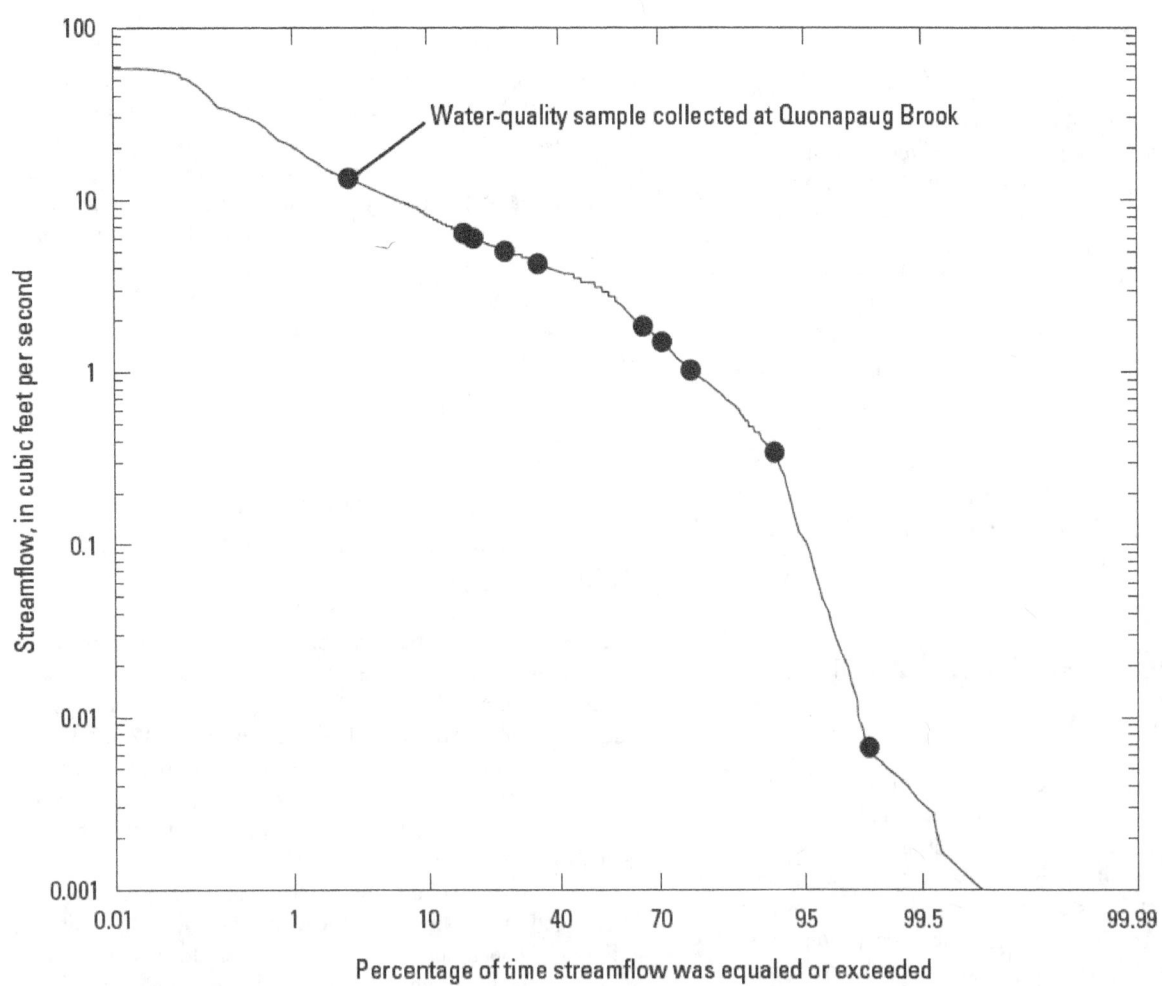

Figure 2.   Flow-duration curve for the U.S. Geological Survey continuous streamgage on Quonapaug Brook at North Scituate (01115183) for water year 2011 and streamflow measurements at this streamgage on the dates (represented by points) when water-quality samples were collected.

Streamflow

Monitoring streamflow is necessary to measure the volume of water and estimate constituent loads to the Scituate Reservoir. The Ponaganset River is the largest monitored tributary to the Scituate Reservoir. Mean daily streamflow at the streamgage on the Ponaganset River (USGS streamgage 01115187) for the entire time period of its operation (mean of the daily mean streamflows for the period of record, WY 1994–2010) prior to WY 2011 was 29 ft³/s (http://waterdata.usgs.gov/nwis). During WY 2011, annual mean streamflow was 37 ft³/s (fig. 3). Mean daily streamflow in Peeptoad Brook (streamgage 01115098), the other long-term continuous-record streamgage in the Scituate Reservoir drainage area, for its period of record (WY 1994–2010) prior to WY 2011 was 11 ft³/s (http://waterdata.usgs.gov/nwis). Annual mean streamflow in Peeptoad Brook during WY 2011 also was 11 ft³/s (table 2).

Water Quality and Constituent Loads and Yields

Water-quality conditions in the Scituate Reservoir drainage area are described by summary statistics for water-quality properties, constituent concentrations, and estimated constituent loads and yields. Loads and yields characterize the rates at which masses of constituents are transferred to the reservoir by tributaries. In the case of loads, tributaries with higher flows tend to have higher loads because the greater volume of water can carry more of the constituent to the reservoir per unit time. Yields represent the constituent load per unit of drainage area and are calculated by dividing the load estimated for a streamgage by the drainage area to the monitoring station. Yields are useful for comparison among streamgages that have different drainage areas because the effects of basin size and therefore total streamflow volume are attenuated. Yields are useful for examining potential differences among basin properties that may contribute to reservoir quality.

Summary statistics include means and medians. For some purposes, median values are more appropriate because they are less likely to be affected by high or low concentrations (or outliers). Medians are especially important to use for summarizing a relatively limited number of values. In contrast, continuously monitored streamflow and sodium and chloride loads (estimated from measurements of specific conductance), which include a large number of values, are better summarized in terms of means because a large dataset is more resistant to the effects of outliers. Mean values also are particularly appropriate for characterizing loads because outlier values, which typically represent large flows, are important to include in estimates of constituent masses delivered to receiving waters.

Sodium and Chloride Loads and Yields Estimated from Specific-Conductance Monitoring Data

Sodium and chloride are constituents of special concern in the Scituate Reservoir drainage area; they are major constituents of road salt used for deicing, and several major roadways cross the drainage basin. State Routes 12 and 14 cut across the main body of the reservoir, and State Route 116 parallels the eastern limb (fig. 1). A recent study by the USGS, in cooperation with the PWSB, indicated that tributaries in basins with state-maintained roads have substantially higher concentrations of sodium and chloride, presumably because of deicing activities (Nimiroski and Waldron, 2002). In addition, sodium is a constituent of potential concern for human health; some persons on restricted diets need to limit their intake of sodium.

Estimated monthly mean[3] sodium concentrations in tributaries of the Scituate Reservoir drainage area ranged from 4.8 to 37.3 mg/L, and estimated monthly mean chloride concentrations ranged from 7.4 to 64.4 mg/L (table 5). The highest monthly mean concentrations of sodium and chloride were measured in Bear Tree Brook (PWSB station number 9) in October 2010 (37.3 and 64.4 mg/L, respectively; table 5).

---

[3] Monthly mean concentrations were calculated by dividing the total monthly load by the total discharge for the month.

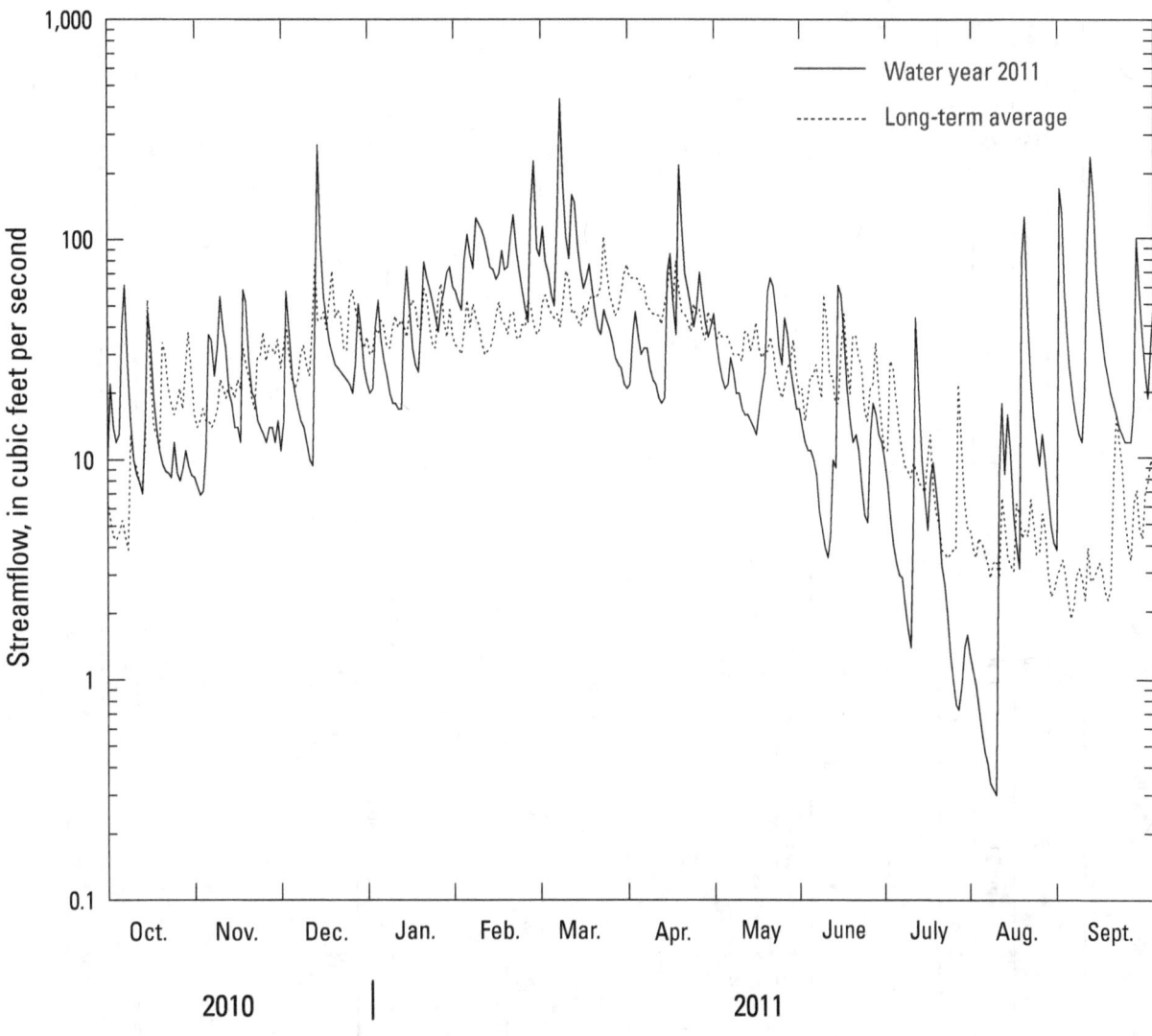

Figure 3.   Measured daily mean streamflow for the U.S. Geological Survey continuous-record streamgage on the Ponaganset River at South Foster (01115187) in the Scituate Reservoir drainage area, Rhode Island, for October 1, 2010, through September 30, 2011, and mean daily streamflow for October 1, 1994, through September 30, 2010.

Table 5. Monthly mean concentrations of chloride and sodium estimated from continuous measurements of specific conductance in the Scituate Reservoir drainage area, Rhode Island, October 1, 2010, through September 30, 2011.

[PWSB, Providence Water Supply Board; USGS, U.S. Geological Survey; Cl, chloride; Na, sodium; monthly mean concentrations were calculated by dividing the monthly load by the total discharge for the month; alternate station names given in parenthesis for stations where different historical names were used for the same sampling location by Providence Water Suply Board]

PWSB station number	USGS station number	Station name	October Cl (mg/L)	October Na (mg/L)	November Cl (mg/L)	November Na (mg/L)	December Cl (mg/L)	December Na (mg/L)	January Cl (mg/L)	January Na (mg/L)	February Cl (mg/L)	February Na (mg/L)	March Cl (mg/L)	March Na (mg/L)
		Barden Reservoir Subbasin												
24	01115190	Dolly Cole Brook	22.5	13.8	21.5	13.2	17.9	11.1	20.8	12.8	25.4	15.5	23.1	14.2
28	01115265	Barden Reservoir (Hemlock Brook)	28.2	17.1	20.4	12.6	15.0	9.37	19.5	12.1	18.5	11.5	16.2	10.1
35	01115187	Ponaganset River	18.8	11.7	18.2	11.3	14.4	9.06	18.1	11.2	21.3	13.1	16.5	10.3
		Direct Runoff Subbasin												
3	01115280	Cork Brook	35.7	21.4	31.6	19.0	21.2	13.0	29.1	17.6	34.6	20.8	27.4	16.6
5	01115184	Spruce Brook	21.8	12.8	18.3	10.9	12.4	7.66	16.4	9.84	17.0	10.2	14.3	8.71
6	01115183	Quonapaug Brook	47.5	28.0	46.6	27.5	32.9	19.8	41.5	24.7	45.0	26.6	38.0	22.7
7	01115297	Wilbur Hollow Brook	15.2	9.20	12.5	7.7	8.59	5.48	9.61	6.07	8.10	5.19	7.98	5.12
8	01115276	Westconnaug Brook (Westconnaug Reservoir)	32.6	19.6	32.8	19.7	18.5	11.5	19.0	11.8	19.4	12.0	17.3	10.8
9	01115275	Bear Tree Brook	64.4	37.3	56.6	33.1	43.7	25.8	51.2	30.1	42.6	25.2	37.6	22.5
		Moswansicut Reservoir Subbasin												
19	01115170	Moswansicut Reservoir (Moswansicut Stream North, Moswansicut Pond)	33.1	19.9	33.2	19.9	32.9	19.8	34.2	20.5	34.4	20.7	33.2	20.0
		Regulating Reservoir												
14	01115110	Huntinghouse Brook	14.8	8.99	10.9	6.80	7.48	4.82	11.9	7.39	10.3	6.44	7.83	5.03
15	01115115	Rush Brook	41.5	24.7	31.1	18.7	21.3	13.0	42.2	25.0	43.2	25.6	31.7	19.1
16	01115098	Peeptoad Brook (Harrisdale Brook)	34.9	20.9	36.7	22.0	29.4	17.8	30.7	18.6	35.9	21.5	30.2	18.2
18	01115120	Unnamed Tributary to Regulating Reservoir (Unnamed Brook A)	32.1	19.3	33.7	20.2	28.1	17.0	46.7	27.6	52.1	30.5	40.4	24.0
		Scituate Reservoir Basin												
		Average	31.7	18.9	28.9	17.3	21.7	13.2	27.9	16.8	29.1	17.5	24.4	14.8

Table 5. Monthly mean concentrations of chloride and sodium estimated from continuous measurements of specific conductance in the Scituate Reservoir drainage area, Rhode Island, October 1, 2010, through September 30, 2011.—Continued

[PWSB, Providence Water Supply Board; USGS, U.S. Geological Survey; Cl, chloride; Na, sodium; monthly mean concentrations were calculated by dividing the monthly load by the total discharge for the month; alternate station names given in parenthesis for stations where different historical names were used for the same sampling location by Providence Water Suply Board]

PWSB station number	USGS station number	Station name	April Cl (mg/L)	April Na (mg/L)	May Cl (mg/L)	May Na (mg/L)	June Cl (mg/L)	June Na (mg/L)	July Cl (mg/L)	July Na (mg/L)	August Cl (mg/L)	August Na (mg/L)	September Cl (mg/L)	September Na (mg/L)
		Barden Reservoir Subbasin												
24	01115190	Dolly Cole Brook	22.8	14.0	23.5	14.4	24.0	14.7	23.6	14.5	20.3	12.5	18.7	11.6
28	01115265	Barden Reservoir (Hemlock Brook)	17.3	10.8	19.0	11.8	19.9	12.3	20.2	12.5	17.0	10.6	14.6	9.17
35	01115187	Ponaganset River	17.2	10.7	18.3	11.3	18.4	11.4	18.3	11.3	15.5	9.70	14.0	8.82
		Direct Runoff Subbasin												
3	01115280	Cork Brook	26.1	15.9	29.3	17.8	29.5	17.9	26.6	16.2	26.1	15.9	20.1	12.4
5	01115184	Spruce Brook	14.8	8.98	16.1	9.68	17.4	10.4	18.3	10.9	19.0	11.3	16.7	10.0
6	01115183	Quonapaug Brook	36.9	22.1	37.2	22.2	36.0	21.5	38.2	22.8	40.0	23.8	35.8	21.4
7	01115297	Wilbur Hollow Brook	9.16	5.81	9.43	5.97	7.44	4.80	8.83	5.62	10.2	6.41	8.38	5.36
8	01115276	Westconnaug Brook (Westconnaug Reservoir)	18.0	11.2	19.7	12.2	21.1	13.0	24.4	14.9	19.4	12.0	17.4	10.8
9	01115275	Bear Tree Brook	40.3	24.0	46.5	27.5	51.9	30.5	59.0	34.4	45.7	26.9	43.7	25.9
		Moswansicut Reservoir Subbasin												
19	01115170	Moswansicut Reservoir (Moswansicut Stream North, Moswansicut Pond)	35.6	21.3	36.6	21.9	36.5	21.8	36.6	21.9	36.7	21.9	35.1	21.1
		Regulating Reservoir Subbasin												
14	01115110	Huntinghouse Brook	9.59	6.05	10.4	6.51	11.4	7.09	12.0	7.41	10.5	6.60	8.80	5.59
15	01115115	Regulating Reservoir (Rush Brook)	29.3	17.7	36.0	21.6	41.1	24.4	34.6	20.7	27.6	16.7	24.8	15.1
16	01115098	Peeptoad Brook (Harrisdale Brook)	34.1	20.5	34.4	20.7	36.9	22.1	38.1	22.8	38.3	22.8	39.3	23.4
18	01115120	Unnamed Tributary to Regulating Reservoir (Unnamed Brook A)	41.3	24.5	47.8	28.2	38.9	23.2	26.6	16.2	29.4	17.8	31.8	19.1
		Scituate Reservoir Basin												
		Average	25.2	15.3	27.4	16.6	27.9	16.8	27.5	16.6	25.4	15.4	23.5	14.3

The highest annual mean[4] concentrations of sodium and chloride also were measured in Bear Tree Brook, 27.0 and 45.8 mg/L, respectively (table 6). These high concentrations are the result of residual sodium and chloride leaching from a formerly uncovered salt storage pile to groundwater (Nimiroski and Waldron, 2002) and relatively small surface-water flows.

The Scituate Reservoir received about 1,600,000 kg (about 1,800 tons) of sodium and 2,600,000 kg (about 2,900 tons) of chloride from tributaries—equipped with instrumentation capable of continuously monitoring specific conductance—during WY 2011. The highest sodium and chloride loads in the watershed during WY 2011—360,000 kg and 580,000 kg, respectively—were measured at the Ponaganset River station (PWSB station number 35; table 6). Monthly estimated sodium and chloride loads were highest in March at 13 stations and in February at 1 station (Ponaganset River; table 7). For these months, the estimated load of sodium and chloride at each station accounted for 12–23 percent of the annual load for each constituent at the respective stations. The highest annual sodium and chloride yields were 53,000 and 90,000 kg/mi[2], respectively, and were measured at Bear Tree Brook (PWSB station number 9; table 6).

Uncertainties associated with measuring streamflow and specific conductance and with sodium and chloride sample collection, preservation, and analysis produce uncertainties in load and yield estimates. The load and yield estimates presented in the text and tables are the most likely values for sodium and chloride coming from tributaries or their drainage basins. It may be best to discuss loads and yields in terms of a range within which the true values lie; however, the most probable values of loads and yields are presented for ease of discussion and presentation. The range within which the true values lie depends on the uncertainties in individual measurements of streamflow and concentration, which are difficult to quantify with available information. The uncertainties associated with estimating streamflow are commonly assumed to affect load and yield calculations more than the errors associated with measuring specific conductance and (or) chemical analysis. The most probable values of loads and yields presented in the tables and text are sufficient for planning-level analysis of water quality in tributaries and their drainage basins.

---

[4] Annual mean concentrations were calculated by dividing the total annual load by the total discharge for the year.

Physical and Chemical Properties and Daily Loads and Yields Estimated from Data Collected by the Providence Water Supply Board

Physical and Chemical Properties

Physical and chemical properties including pH, turbidity, alkalinity, specific conductance, and color were routinely measured to characterize water quality from each basin (table 8). Specifically, pH is a measure of the acidity of the water, color can be an indirect measure of the amount of organic carbon dissolved in the water column, turbidity is an indirect measure of suspended particles, and alkalinity is a measure of the acid-neutralizing capacity of water.

The median pH in tributaries in the Scituate Reservoir drainage area ranged from 5.6 to 6.8; the median of the medians for all stations was 6.2. Median values of color ranged from 12 to 210 platinum cobalt units (PCU); the median for all stations was 55 PCU. Median values of turbidity ranged from 0.21 to 1.9 nephelometric turbidity units (NTU); the median for all stations was 0.68 NTU. Median alkalinity values in tributaries were low, ranging from 2.5 to 15 mg/L as $CaCO_3$; the median for all stations was 4.9 mg/L as $CaCO_3$ (table 8).

Constituent Concentrations and Daily Loads and Yields

Fecal indicator bacteria, chloride, and nutrients such as phosphorus and nitrogen are commonly detected in natural water; at elevated concentrations, these constituents can render water unfit for the intended use. Fecal indicator bacteria, which are found in the intestines of warm-blooded animals, may indicate impairment from sewage contamination or from livestock or wildlife that defecate in or near the stream margin. Chloride originates in tributary streamwater from precipitation, weathering, or human activities such as waste disposal, use of septic systems, and road deicing. Sources of nutrients in tributary streamwater include atmospheric deposition, leaching of naturally occurring organic material, discharge of groundwater that is enriched in nutrients from septic-system leachate, and runoff contaminated with fertilizer or animal waste. The ultimate intended use of water in the tributaries is drinking water, which must meet specific water-quality standards. For this reason, the PWSB and the USGS closely monitor concentrations of these constituents in tributaries. Median concentrations, loads, and yields of water-quality constituents are given in tables 8 and 9.

Table 6. Annual mean chloride and sodium concentrations, loads, and yields by sampling station in the Scituate Reservoir drainage area, Rhode Island, October 1, 2010, through September 30, 2011.

[PWSB, Providence Water Supply Board; USGS, U.S. Geological Survey; no., number; mg/L, milligrams per liter; kg, kilograms; kg/mi², kilograms per square mile; Cl, chloride; Na, sodium; annual mean concentrations were calculated by dividing the annual load by the total discharge for the year; alternate station names given in parenthesis for stations where different historical names were used for the same sampling location by Providence Water Supply Board]

PWSB station no.	USGS station no.	Station name	Concentration		Load		Yield	
			Cl (mg/L)	Na (mg/L)	Cl (kg)	Na (kg)	Cl (kg/mi²)	Na (kg/mi²)
Barden Reservoir Subbasin								
24	01115190	Dolly Cole Brook	22.1	13.6	220,000	140,000	45,000	28,000
28	01115265	Barden Reservoir (Hemlock Brook)	17.6	10.9	330,000	200,000	38,000	23,000
35	01115187	Ponaganset River	17.5	10.9	580,000	360,000	41,000	26,000
Direct Runoff Subbasin								
3	01115280	Cork Brook	27.1	16.4	82,000	50,000	46,000	28,000
5	01115184	Spruce Brook	15.7	9.47	32,000	19,000	26,000	16,000
6	01115183	Quonapaug Brook	38.9	23.2	140,000	83,000	71,000	42,000
7	01115297	Wilbur Hollow Brook	9.16	5.80	67,000	42,000	15,000	9,800
8	01115276	Westconnaug Brook (Westconnaug Reservoir)	19.7	12.2	130,000	81,000	25,000	16,000
9	01115275	Bear Tree Brook	45.8	27.0	56,000	33,000	90,000	53,000
Moswansicut Reservoir Subbasin								
19	01115170	Moswansicut Reservoir, (Moswansicut Stream North, Moswansicut Pond)	34.7	20.8	190,000	120,000	60,000	36,000
Regulating Reservoir Subbasin								
14	01115110	Huntinghouse Brook	9.50	5.99	110,000	71,000	18,000	11,000
15	01115115	Rush Brook	32.2	19.3	280,000	170,000	59,000	35,000
16	01115098	Peeptoad Brook (Harrisdale Brook)	33.7	20.3	330,000	200,000	67,000	40,000
18	01115120	Unnamed Tributary to Regulating Reservoir (Unnamed Brook A)	40.0	23.8	18,000	11,000	64,000	38,000
Scituate Reservoir Basin								
			Average		Total		Average	
			26.0	15.7	2,600,000	1,600,000	48,000	29,000

Table 7. Monthly estimated chloride and sodium loads by sampling station in the Scituate Reservoir drainage area Rhode Island, October 1, 2010, through September 30, 2011.

[PWSB, Providence Water Supply Board; USGS, U.S. Geological Survey; no., number, Cl, chloride; Na, sodium; kg, kilogram; alternate station names given in parenthesis for stations where different historical names were used for the same sampling location by Providence Water Supply Board]

PWSB station number	USGS station number	Station name	October Cl (Kg)	October Na (Kg)	November Cl (Kg)	November Na (Kg)	December Cl (Kg)	December Na (Kg)	January Cl (Kg)	January Na (Kg)	February Cl (Kg)	February Na (Kg)	March Cl (Kg)	March Na (Kg)
		Barden Reservoir Subbasin												
24	01115190	Dolly Cole Brook	7,200	4,400	13,000	8,200	19,000	12,000	18,000	11,000	41,000	25,000	44,000	27,000
28	01115265	Barden Reservoir (Hemlock Brook)	14,000	8,700	17,000	10,000	25,000	16,000	30,000	19,000	41,000	25,000	56,000	35,000
35	01115187	Ponaganset River	23,000	14,000	29,000	18,000	40,000	25,000	59,000	37,000	130,000	81,000	98,000	61,000
		Direct Runoff Subbasin												
3	01115280	Cork Brook	2,300	1,400	4,400	2,700	7,200	4,400	6,500	4,000	10,000	6,200	16,000	9,500
5	01115184	Spruce Brook	810	480	1,300	780	2,700	1,600	2,400	1,400	3,300	2,000	6,100	3,700
6	01115183	Quonapaug Brook	5,900	3,500	9,600	5,700	13,000	7,700	12,000	7,400	18,000	11,000	25,000	15,000
7	01115297	Wilbur Hollow Brook	4,400	2,700	5,000	3,100	6,300	4,000	5,000	3,200	6,300	4,000	9,700	6,200
8	01115276	Westconnaug Brook (Westconnaug Reservoir)	5,900	3,600	6,700	4,000	9,400	5,800	11,000	6,700	12,000	7,500	16,000	10,000
9	01115275	Bear Tree Brook	2,900	1,700	3,100	1,800	4,400	2,600	4,200	2,400	4,300	2,500	7,200	4,300
		Moswansicut Reservoir Subbasin												
19	01115170	Moswansicut Reservoir (Moswansicut Stream North, Moswansicut Pond)	5,800	3,500	9,700	5,800	18,000	11,000	15,000	9,000	17,000	10,000	34,000	21,000
		Regulating Reservoir												
14	01115110	Huntinghouse Brook	3,500	2,100	5,900	3,700	9,500	6,100	8,600	5,300	16,000	10,000	21,000	13,000
15	01115115	Rush Brook	9,000	5,300	14,000	8,500	20,000	12,000	23,000	14,000	45,000	27,000	51,000	31,000
16	01115098	Peeptoad Brook (Harrisdale Brook)	14,000	8,400	28,000	17,000	38,000	23,000	19,000	11,000	39,000	24,000	69,000	42,000
18	01115120	Unnamed Tributary to Regulating Reservoir (Unnamed Brook A)	240	150	330	200	1,300	760	1,700	1,000	3,100	1,800	4,200	2,500
		Scituate Reservoir Basin												
		Total	99,000	60,000	150,000	89,000	210,000	130,000	220,000	130,000	390,000	240,000	460,000	280,000

Table 7. Monthly estimated chloride and sodium loads by sampling station in the Scituate Reservoir drainage area Rhode Island, October 1, 2010, through September 30, 2011.—Continued

[PWSB, Providence Water Supply Board; USGS, U.S. Geological Survey; no., number; Cl, chloride; Na, sodium; kg, kilogram; alternate station names given in parenthesis for stations where different historical names were used for the same sampling location by Providence Water Supply Board]

PWSB station number	USGS station number	Station name	April Cl (Kg)	April Na (Kg)	May Cl (Kg)	May Na (Kg)	June Cl (Kg)	June Na (Kg)	July Cl (Kg)	July Na (Kg)	August Cl (Kg)	August Na (Kg)	September Cl (Kg)	September Na (Kg)
		Barden Reservoir Subbasin												
24	01115190	Dolly Cole Brook	28,000	17,000	13,000	8,000	6,000	3,700	3,000	1,800	13,000	8,100	15,000	9,600
28	01115265	Barden Reservoir (Hemlock Brook)	39,000	24,000	25,000	15,000	15,000	9,400	6,700	4,100	26,000	16,000	32,000	20,000
35	01115187	Ponaganset River	63,000	39,000	36,000	23,000	19,000	12,000	7,200	4,500	31,000	19,000	43,000	27,000
		Direct Runoff Subbasin												
3	01115280	Cork Brook	11,000	6,700	6,600	4,000	3,100	1,900	1,900	1,200	6,600	4,000	6,200	3,800
5	01115184	Spruce Brook	4,700	2,900	3,200	1,900	1,700	1,000	1,100	630	1,600	940	2,800	1,700
6	01115183	Quonapaug Brook	18,000	11,000	12,000	7,000	5,100	3,000	1,700	1,000	6,900	4,100	12,000	7,300
7	01115297	Wilbur Hollow Brook	9,100	5,800	6,400	4,100	2,600	1,600	820	520	4,400	2,700	7,000	4,500
8	01115276	Westconnaug Brook (Westconnaug Reservoir)	15,000	9,400	15,000	9,500	11,000	6,500	6,400	3,900	8,400	5,200	14,000	8,500
9	01115275	Bear Tree Brook	6,300	3,800	5,600	3,300	4,300	2,500	3,300	1,900	4,200	2,500	5,700	3,400
		Moswansicut Reservoir Subbasin												
19	01115170	Moswansicut Reservoir (Moswansicut Stream North, Moswansicut Pond)	28,000	17,000	19,000	11,000	11,000	6,500	6,000	3,600	11,000	6,600	19,000	11,000
		Regulating Reservoir Subbasin												
14	01115110	Huntinghouse Brook	17,000	11,000	9,600	6,000	4,600	2,900	1,600	1,000	6,500	4,100	9,300	5,900
15	01115115	Regulating Reservoir (Rush Brook)	37,000	22,000	24,000	14,000	11,000	6,400	4,800	2,900	17,000	10,000	22,000	13,000
16	01115098	Peeptoad Brook (Harrisdale Brook)	34,000	21,000	13,000	7,600	15,000	8,900	4,300	2,600	26,000	15,000	34,000	20,000
18	01115120	Unnamed Tributary to Regulating Reservoir (Unnamed Brook A)	3,000	1,800	1,500	910	530	320	230	140	690	420	1,300	760
		Scituate Reservoir Basin												
		Total	310,000	190,000	190,000	120,000	110,000	67,000	49,000	30,000	160,000	99,000	220,000	140,000

Table 8. Median values for water-quality data collected at Providence Water Supply Board stations, by tributary reservoir subbasin in the Scituate Reservoir drainage area Rhode Island, October 1, 2010, through September 30, 2011.

[Water-quality data are from samples collected and analyzed by Providence Water (PWSB); no., number; USGS, U.S. Geological Survey; PCU, platinum cobalt units; NTU, nephelometric turbidity units; CFU/100mL, colony forming units per 100 milliliters; E. coli, Escherichia coli; mg/L, milligrams per liter; CaCO₃, calcium carbonate; N, nitrogen; P, phosphorus; <, less than; >, greater than; --, no data; alternate station names given in parenthesis for stations where different historical names were used for the same sampling location by Providence Water]

PWSB station no.	USGS station no.	Station name	pH (units)	Color (PCU)	Turbidity (NTU)	Total coliform bacteria (CFU/100mL)	E. coli (CFU/100mL)	Alkalinity (mg/L as CaCO₃)	Chloride (mg/L)	Nitrite (mg/L as N)	Nitrate (mg/L as N)	Orthophosphate (mg/L as P)
Barden Reservoir Subbasin												
24	01115190	Dolly Cole Brook	6.1	68	0.78	23	14	4.5	26	0.002	0.01	0.07
25	01115200	Shippee Brook	6.0	45	0.75	23	23	3.1	15	0.002	<0.01	0.05
26	01115185	Windsor Brook	6.2	44	0.43	240	23	2.8	16	0.001	0.01	0.15
27	01115845	Unnamed Tributary to Ponaganset River (Unnamed Brook B, Unnamed Brook West of Windsor Brook)	5.8	21	0.25	12	2.8	4.6	14	0.001	<0.01	0.02
28	01115265	Barden Reservoir (Hemlock Brook)	5.8	80	0.63	1,100	310	2.8	20	0.003	<0.01	0.08
29	01115271	Ponaganset River (Barden Stream)	6.1	55	0.78	23	23	4.1	20	0.002	<0.01	0.08
35	01115187	Ponaganset River	6.2	72	0.64	23	23	4.1	19	0.002	<0.01	0.08
Direct Runoff Subbasin												
1	01115180	Brandy Brook	6.7	70	1.2	150	21	9.4	12	0.002	0.01	0.1
2	01115181	Unnamed Tributary #2 to Scituate Reservoir (Unnamed Brook North of Bullhead Brook)	6.3	18	0.26	23	23	3.4	14	0.001	0.03	0.07
3	01115280	Cork Brook	6.3	45	0.4	>2,400	240	4.9	30	0.002	0.01	0.05
4	01115400	Kent Brook (Betty Pond Stream)	6.3	32	0.68	23	1.5	7.6	5.7	0.001	<0.01	0.05
5	01115184	Spruce Brook	6.0	70	0.43	23	23	4.2	19	0.002	0.01	0.06
6	01115183	Quonapaug Brook	6.4	84	1	43	43	8.8	38	0.002	<0.01	0.1
7	01115297	Wilbur Hollow Brook	6.1	85	0.84	1,100	33	5.9	16	0.003	<0.01	0.08
8	01115276	Westconnaug Brook (Westconnaug Reservoir)	6.1	18	0.59	23	23	3.5	19	0.001	0.01	0.08
9	01115275	Bear Tree Brook	6.4	48	0.35	58	6.5	5.4	34	0.002	0.04	0.07
30	01115350	Unnamed Tributary #4 to Scituate Reservoir (Coventry Brook, Knight Brook)	6.0	57	0.37	33	23	4	24	0.002	0.02	0.07
31	1115177	Toad Pond	6.5	45	0.78	93	23	4.9	87	0.002	0.13	0.08
32	01115178	Unnamed Tributary #1 to Scituate Reservoir (Pine Swamp Brook)	6.3	65	0.74	23	23	4.9	15	0.001	0.01	0.09
33	01115182	Unnamed Tributary #3 to Scituate Reservoir (Hall's Estate Brook)	6.2	55	0.48	240	20	2.9	19	0.002	0.03	0.04
36	--	Outflow from King Pond	6.2	20	0.26	23	4	3.4	5.1	0.001	0.01	0.04
37	--	Fire Tower Stream	5.8	44	0.28	4	4	3.8	4.6	0.001	0.03	0.03

Table 8. Median values for water-quality data collected at Providence Water Supply Board stations, by tributary reservoir subbasin in the Scituate Reservoir drainage area Rhode Island, October 1, 2010, through September 30, 2011.—Continued

[Water-quality data are from samples collected and analyzed by Providence Water (PWSB); no., number; USGS, U.S. Geological Survey; PCU, platinum cobalt units; NTU, nephelometric turbidity units; CFU/100mL, colony forming units per 100 milliliters; E. coli, Escherichia coli; mg/L, milligrams per liter; CaCO3, calcium carbonate; N, nitrogen; P, phosphorus; <, less than; >, greater than; --, no data; alternate station names given in parenthesis for stations where different historical names were used for the same sampling location by Providence Water]

PWSB station no.	USGS station no.	Station name	Properties					Constituents				
			pH (units)	Color (PCU)	Turbidity (NTU)	Total coliform bacteria (CFU/100mL)	E. coli (CFU/100mL)	Alkalinity (mg/L as CaCO3)	Chloride (mg/L)	Nitrite (mg/L as N)	Nitrate (mg/L as N)	Orthophosphate (mg/L as P)
		Moswansicut Reservoir Subbasin										
19	01115170	Moswansicut Reservoir (Moswansicut Stream North, Moswansicut Pond)	6.8	28	1.2	23	4	7	32	0.001	0.01	0.06
20	01115160	Unnamed Tributary #1 to Moswansicut Reservoir (Blanchard Brook)	6.1	210	0.93	350	240	7.9	43	0.003	0.01	0.13
21	01115165	Unnamed Tributary #2 to Moswansicut Reservoir (Brook from Kimball Reservoir)	6.6	85	1.4	630	29	6	19	0.003	0.03	0.06
22	01115167	Moswansicut Reservoir (Moswansicut Stream South)	6.6	60	1.9	1,100	1,100	15	40	0.005	0.06	0.15
34	01115164	Kimball Stream	6.5	65	0.57	23	9	8.8	31	0.002	<0.01	0.06
		Ponaganset Reservoir Subbasin										
23	011151843	Ponaganset Reservoir	6.0	12	0.46	12	1.5	2.6	12	0.001	0.01	0.03
		Regulating Reservoir Subbasin										
13	01115176	Regulating Reservoir	6.7	29	0.76	9	4	3.7	30	0.001	<0.01	0.06
14	01115110	Huntinghouse Brook	6.5	47	0.74	200	84	9.6	8.9	0.002	<0.01	0.08
15	01115115	Rush Brook	6.6	74	0.8	150	39	13	35	0.002	0.01	0.07
16	01115098	Peeptoad Brook (Harrisdale Brook)	6.5	42	0.98	75	39	10	34	0.001	0.01	0.06
17	01115119	Dexter Pond (Paine Pond)	5.9	60	0.6	120	5.3	5	33	0.002	<0.01	0.11
18	01115120	Unnamed Tributary to Regulating Reservoir (Unnamed Brook A)	6.5	70	0.76	>2,400	43	8.9	43	0.002	0.01	0.07
		Westconnaug Reservoir Subbasin										
10	01115274	Westconnaug Brook	5.6	33	0.21	110	19	2.5	23	0.001	<0.01	0.065
11	01115273	Unnamed Tributary to Westconnaug Reservoir (Unnamed Brook South of Westconnaug Reservoir)	5.7	100	0.64	23	23	4.1	32	0.005	0.03	0.035
12	011152745	Unnamed Tributary to Westconnaug Brook (Unnamed Brook north of Westconnaug Reservoir)	6.2	62	0.69	23	23	4.9	6.1	0.003	0.05	0.03
		Scituate Reservoir Basin										
		Minimum	5.6	12	0.21	4	1.5	2.5	4.6	0.001	<0.01	0.02
		Median	6.2	55	0.68	33	23	4.9	20	0.002	0.01	0.07
		Maximum	6.8	210	1.9	>2,400	1,100	15	87	0.005	0.13	0.15

Table 9. Median daily loads and yields of bacteria, chloride, nitrite, nitrate, and orthophosphate by tributary reservoir subbasin, in the Scituate Reservoir drainage area Rhode Island, October 1, 2010, through September 30, 2011.

[Water-quality data are from samples collected and analyzed by Providence Water Supply Board (PWSB); USGS, U.S. Geological Survey; CFUx10⁶/d; millions of colony forming units per day; *E. coli*, *Escherichia coli*; N, nitrogen; P, phosphorus; kg/d, kilograms per day; kg/d/mi², kilograms per day per square mile; g/d, grams per day; g/d/mi², grams per day per square mile; alternate station names given in parenthesis for stations where different historical names were used for the same sampling location by Providence Water]

PWSB station number	USGS station number	Station name	Total coliform bacteria (CFU×10⁶/d)	Total coliform bacteria (CFU×10⁶/mi²)	E. Coli (CFU×10⁶/d)	E. Coli (CFU×10⁶/mi²)	Chloride (kg/d)	Chloride (kg/d/mi²)	Nitrite (as N) (g/d)	Nitrite (as N) (g/d/mi²)	Nitrate (as N) (g/d)	Nitrate (as N) (g/d/mi²)	Orthophosphate (as P) (g/d)	Orthophosphate (as P) (g/d/mi²)
Barden Reservoir Subbasin														
24	01115190	Dolly Cole Brook	3,100	630	2,200	440	360	73	25	5.1	110	23	1,100	220
25	01115200	Shippee Brook	3,200	1,400	1,900	810	230	98	31	13	110	47	630	270
26	01115185	Windsor Brook	75,000	17,000	4,000	920	300	69	28	6.5	200	46	4,600	1,100
28	01115265	Barden Reservoir (Hemlock Brook)	290,000	33,000	160,000	18,000	770	88	92	10	220	25	2,900	330
35	01115187	Ponaganset River	11,000	790	11,000	790	1,400	100	88	6.3	490	35	3,600	260
Direct Runoff Subbasin														
1	01115180	Brandy Brook	6,700	4,300	1,400	890	73	46	9	6	28	18	610	390
3	01115280	Cork Brook	>65,000	>36,000	65,000	36,000	76	42	5.4	3	54	30	200	110
4	01115400	Kent Brook	850	1,000	320	380	15	18	2.2	2.6	22	26	170	200
5	01115184	Spruce Brook	2,800	2,300	490	400	36	30	2.3	1.9	13	11	92	75
6	01115183	Quonapaug Brook	4,600	2,300	4,400	2,200	310	160	14	7.1	81	41	730	370
7	01115297	Wilbur Hollow Brook	210,000	48,000	4,700	1,100	290	67	41	9.4	130	29	1,200	280
8	01115276	Westconnaug Brook	1,800	350	1,600	310	390	75	24	4.6	120	23	820	160
9	01115275	Bear Tree Brook	1,200	1,900	170	270	140	230	6.7	11	200	320	230	370
32	01115178	Unnamed Tributary #1 to Scituate Reservoir (Pine Swamp Brook)	570	1,300	100	220	38	84	2.5	5.6	25	56	220	490
33	01115182	Unnamed Tributary #3 to Scituate Reservoir (Hall's Estate Brook)	700	2,500	70	250	16	56	1.2	4.1	25	88	34	120
Moswansicut Reservoir Subbasin														
19	01115170	Moswansicut Reservoir (Moswansicut Stream North, Moswansicut Pond)	2,800	860	770	240	260	80	10	3	61	19	430	130

Table 9. Median daily loads and yields of bacteria, chloride, nitrite, nitrate, and orthophosphate by tributary reservoir subbasin, in the Scituate Reservoir drainage area Rhode Island, October 1, 2010, through September 30, 2011.—Continued

[Water-quality data are from samples collected and analyzed by Providence Water Supply Board (PWSB); USGS, U.S. Geological Survey; CFUx10⁶/d; millions of colony forming units per day; *E. coli*, *Escherichia coli*; N, nitrogen; P, phosphorus; kg/d, kilograms per day; kg/d/mi², kilograms per day per square mile; g/d, grams per day; g/d/mi², grams per day per square mile; alternate station names given in parenthesis for stations where different historical names were used for the same sampling location by Providence Water]

PWSB station number	USGS station number	Station name	Total coliform bacteria		E. Coli		Chloride		Nitrite (as N)		Nitrate (as N)		Orthophosphate (as P)	
			(CFUx10⁶/d)	(CFUx10⁶/mi²)	(CFUx10⁶/d)	(CFUx10⁶/mi²)	(kg/d)	(kg/d/mi²)	(g/d)	(g/d/mi²)	(g/d)	(g/d/mi²)	(g/d)	(g/d/mi²)
21	01115165	Unnamed Tributary #2 to Moswansicut Reservoir (Brook from Kimball Reservoir)	31,000	110,000	1,200	4,200	85	290	5.7	20	140	480	140	490
		Regulating Reservoir												
14	01115110	Huntinghouse Brook	25,000	3,900	16,000	2,500	250	39	40	6.4	160	25	2,300	360
15	01115115	Rush Brook	26,000	5,500	2,600	550	650	140	30	6.4	120	26	1,000	210
16	01115098	Peeptoad Brook (Harrisdale Brook)	18,000	3,600	4,200	850	570	110	22	4.4	120	24	720	150
18	01115120	Unnamed Tributary to Regulating Reservoir (Unnamed Brook A)	>100,000	>350,000	1,800	6,400	180	640	8	30	42	150	290	1,000
		Westconnaug Reservoir Subbasin												
10	01115274	Westconnaug Brook	4,000	2,700	700	470	120	78	4.6	3.1	26	18	400	270
11	01115273	Unnamed Tributary to Westconnaug Reservoir (Unnamed Brook South of Westconnaug Reservoir)	620	860	620	860	120	170	7	9.7	150	200	43	59
		Scituate Reservoir Basin												
		Minimum	570	350	70	220	15	18	1.2	1.9	13	11	34	59
		Median	4,300	2,500	1,800	810	230	80	10	6.3	110	29	610	270
		Maximum	290,000	>350,000	160,000	36,000	1,400	640	92	30	490	480	4,600	1,100

Bacteria

Median concentrations of total coliform and *E. coli* bacteria were above the detection limit (3 CFU/100 mL) at nearly all sites (table 8). Total coliform bacteria concentrations were in most cases equal to or greater than *E. coli* concentrations (as expected because total coliform is more inclusive); the median concentrations for all sites in the drainage basin were equal to 33 CFU/100 mL for total coliform bacteria and 23 CFU/100 mL for *E. coli* bacteria. Median concentrations of total coliform bacteria were highest at Cork Brook (PWSB station number 3; table 8) and at Unnamed Tributary to Regulating Reservoir (PWSB station number 18; table 8) at more than 2,400 CFU/100 mL. Median concentrations of *E. coli* bacteria were highest at Moswansicut Reservoir (PWSB station number 22; table 8) at 1,100 CFU/100 mL.

Concentrations of fecal indicator bacteria were lowest at sampling stations Regulating Reservoir (PWSB station number 13), Ponaganset Reservoir (PWSB station number 23), Unnamed Tributary to Ponaganset River (PWSB station number 27), and Fire Tower Stream (PWSB station number 37). In addition to these sampling stations, concentrations of *E. coli* bacteria also were relatively low at Dexter Pond (PWSB station number 17), Moswansicut Reservoir (PWSB station number 19), and Outflow from King Pond (PWSB station number 36). Median daily loads and yields of total coliform and *E. coli* bacteria varied by about three orders of magnitude; the highest median daily yield of total coliform bacteria was at Unnamed Tributary to Regulating Reservoir (PWSB station number 18; table 9), and the highest median daily yield of *E. coli* bacteria was at Cork Brook (PWSB station number 3; table 9). Although relatively high for sampling stations in the Scituate Reservoir Subbasin, median daily bacteria yields at this station are low to moderate compared to yields of indicator bacteria in sewage-contaminated streamwater or streamwater affected by stormwater runoff in an urban environment (Breault and others, 2002). The median daily loads of total coliform bacteria for all subbasins in the Scituate Reservoir drainage area ranged from 570 to 290,000 CFUx10⁶/d, and yields ranged from 350 to greater than 350,000 CFUx10⁶/d/mi²; *E coli* loads ranged from 70 to 160,000 CFUx10⁶/d, and yields ranged from 220 to 36,000 CFUx10⁶/d/mi² (table 9). These median daily loads were substantially greater than the values in the previous water year, when the median daily loads of total coliform bacteria ranged from 360 to 29,000 CFUx10⁶/d, and loads of *E coli* bacteria ranged from 57 to 8,700 CFUx10⁶/d (Smith and Breault, 2011).

Chloride

The highest median chloride concentration (87.0 mg/L) was measured in the Direct Runoff Subbasin at Toad Pond (PWSB station number 31; table 8). Median daily chloride loads and yields estimated from samples collected by the PWSB varied among monitoring stations in the drainage area (table 9); the median chloride yield for the overall drainage area was about 80 kilograms per day per square mile (kg/d/mi²). Ponaganset River (PWSB station number 35) had the largest median daily chloride load (1,400 kilograms per day (kg/d)). The largest median daily chloride yield (640 kg/d/mi²) was determined for Unnamed Tributary to Regulating Reservoir (PWSB station number 18); this yield is greater than the mean daily chloride yield [64,000 kilograms per year per square mile (kg/yr/mi²) (table 6) or about 175 kg/d/mi²] estimated for that station by using continuously measured specific-conductance records. The mean annual yield of chloride and sodium for the drainage areas above the 14 USGS continuous-record streamgages, which represent nearly 66 percent of the Scituate watershed, was 113 kg/d/mi² and 70 kg/d/mi², respectively.

Nutrients

Median concentrations of nitrite and nitrate (table 8) were 0.002 and 0.01 mg/L as nitrogen (N), respectively. Higher concentrations of nitrite and nitrate at some monitoring sites, such as Moswansicut Reservoir (PWSB station number 22) in the Moswansicut Reservoir Subbasin (0.005 mg/L as N and 0.06 mg/L as N, respectively), may have been affected by nutrient-enriched runoff or groundwater (Nimiroski and others, 2008). The median concentration of orthophosphate for the entire study area (table 8) was 0.07 mg/L as P. The maximum median concentration of orthophosphate (0.15 mg/L as P) was measured in Windsor Brook (PWSB station number 26). Median daily nutrient loads from the Ponaganset River (PWSB station number 35) into the Scituate Reservoir—nitrite (88 g/d), nitrate (490 g/d), and orthophosphate (4,600 g/d)—were among the largest for all the sampled stations. Median daily nitrite loads for WY 2011 were larger at only one station, Barden Reservoir (PWSB station number 28; 92 g/d). The largest median daily yield for nitrite (30 g/d/mi²) was determined for Unnamed Tributary to Regulating Reservoir (PWSB station number 18). The largest median daily yield for nitrate (480 g/d/mi²) was determined for Unnamed Tributary 2 to Moswansicut Reservoir (PWSB station number 21), and the largest median daily yield for orthophosphate (1,100 g/d/mi²) was determined for Windsor Brook (PWSB station number 26; table 9). The median daily yield for orthophosphate for Unnamed Tributary to Regulating Reservoir (PWSB station number 18; 1,000 g/d/mi²) also was high compared with the other stations in the monitoring network.

References Cited

Breault, R.F., 2010, Streamflow, water quality, and constituent loads and yields, Scituate Reservoir drainage area, Rhode Island, water year 2002: U.S. Geological Survey Open-File Report 2009–1041, 25 p.

Breault, R.F., and Campbell, J.P., 2010a, Streamflow, water quality, and constituent loads and yields, Scituate Reservoir drainage area, Rhode Island, water year 2003: U.S. Geological Survey Open-File Report 2010–1043, 24 p.

Breault, R.F., and Campbell, J.P., 2010b, Streamflow, water quality, and constituent loads and yields, Scituate Reservoir drainage area, Rhode Island, Water Year 2004: U.S. Geological Survey Open-File Report 2010–1044, 24 p.

Breault, R.F., and Campbell, J.P., 2010c, Streamflow, water quality, and constituent loads and yields, Scituate Reservoir drainage area, Rhode Island, water year 2005: U.S. Geological Survey Open-File Report 2010–1045, 24 p.

Breault, R.F., and Campbell, J.P., 2010d, Streamflow, water quality, and constituent loads and yields, Scituate Reservoir drainage area, Rhode Island, water year 2006: U.S. Geological Survey Open-File Report 2010–1046, 25 p.

Breault, R.F., and Smith, K.P., 2010, Streamflow, water quality, and constituent loads and yields, Scituate Reservoir drainage area, Rhode Island, water year 2009: U.S. Geological Survey Open-File Report 2010–1275, 24 p.

Breault, R.F., Waldron, M.C., Barlow, L.K., and Dickerman, D.C., 2000, Water-quality conditions in relation to drainage basin characteristics in the Scituate Reservoir Basin, Rhode Island, 1982–95: U.S. Geological Survey Water-Resources Investigations Report 00–4086, 46 p.

Breault, R.F., Sorenson, J.R., and Weiskel, P.K., 2002, Streamflow, water quality, and contaminant loads in the lower Charles River watershed, Massachusetts, 1999–2000: U.S. Geological Survey Water-Resources Investigations Report 02–4137, 131 p.

Helsel, D.R., and Hirsch, R.M., 1992, Statistical methods in water resources: New York, Elsevier, Studies in Environmental Science 49, 522 p.

Hirsch, R.M., 1982, A comparison of four streamflow record extension techniques: Water Resources Research, v. 18, no. 4, p. 1081–1088.

Hirsch, R.M., and Gilroy, E.J., 1984, Methods of fitting a straight line to data—Examples in water resources: Water Resources Bulletin, v. 20, no. 5, p. 705–711.

National Institute of Standards and Technology/ SEmiconductor MAnufacturing TECHnology, 2012, NIST/ SEMATECH e-Handbook of Statistical Methods: U.S. Department of Commerce, accessed April 17, 2013, at http://www.itl.nist.gov/div898/handbook/.

Nimiroski, M.T., and Waldron, M.C., 2002, Sources of sodium and chloride in the Scituate Reservoir drainage basin, Rhode Island: U.S. Geological Survey Water-Resources Investigations Report 02–4149, 16 p.

Nimiroski, M.T., DeSimone, L.A., and Waldron, M.C., 2008, Water-quality conditions and constituent loads, 1996–2002, and water-quality trends, 1983–2002, in the Scituate Reservoir drainage area, Rhode Island: U.S. Geological Survey Scientific Investigations Report 2008–5060, 55 p.

Providence Water Supply Board Water Quality Laboratory, 2003, Quality Assurance Program Manual: Providence Water Supply Board, variously paged.

Ries, K.G., III, and Friesz, P.J., 2000, Methods for estimating low-flow statistics for Massachusetts streams: U.S. Geological Survey Water-Resources Investigations Report 00–4136, 81 p.

Smith, K.P. and Breault, R.F., 2011, Streamflow, water quality, and constituent loads and yields, Scituate Reservoir drainage area, Rhode Island, water year 2010: U.S. Geological Survey Open-File Report 2011–1076, 20 p.

Tasker, G.D., and Driver, N.E., 1988, Nationwide regression models for predicting urban runoff water quality at unmonitored sites: Water Resources Bulletin, v. 24, no. 5, p. 1090–1101.

U.S. Geological Survey, 2001, National Water Information System data available on the World Wide Web (Water Data for the Nation): U.S. Geological Survey, accessed November 10, 2010, at http://waterdata.usgs.gov/nwis/.

U.S. Geological Survey, 2007, Water-resources data for the United States, Water Year 2006: U.S. Geological Survey Water-Data Report WDR–US–2006, accessed November 5, 2009, at http://wdr.water.usgs.gov/.

Wagner, R.J., Boulger, R.W., Jr., Oblinger, C.J., and Smith, B.A., 2006, Guidelines and standard procedures for continuous water-quality monitors—Station operation, record computation, and data reporting: U.S. Geological Survey Techniques and Methods 1–D3, 51 p., 8 attachments, accessed April 10, 2006, at http://pubs.water.usgs.gov/tm1d3.

Table 4. Daily loads of bacteria, chloride, nitrite, nitrate, and orthophosphate by tributary reservoir subbasin in the Scituate Reservoir drainage area, Rhode Island, October 1, 2010, through September 30, 2011.

[Water-quality data are from samples collected and analyzed by Providence Water Supply Board (PWSB); USGS, U.S. Geological Survey; ft³/s, cubic feet per second; CFU×10⁶/d, millions of colony forming units per day; *E. coli, Escherichia coli*; kg/d, kilograms per day; g/d, grams per day; N, nitrogen; P, phosphorus; <, less than; >, greater than; shaded areas indicate values that were calculated with concentration data censored at half the detection level; alternate station names given in parenthesis for stations where different historical names were used for the same sampling location by Providence Water Supply Board]

PWSB station number	USGS station number	Station name	Date	Daily mean streamflow (ft³/s)	Total coliform bacteria (CFU×10⁶/d)	E. Coli (CFU×10⁶/d)	Chloride (kg/d)	Nitrite (g/d as N)	Nitrate (g/d as N)	Orthophos-phate (g/d as P)
					Barden Reservoir Subbasin					
24	01115190	Dolly Cole Brook	10/29/10	1.4	51	51	52	10	68	34
			11/05/10	5.6	63,000	63,000	300	41	68	1,200
			12/03/10	21	48,000	48,000	1,200	100	260	2,600
			01/07/11	5.7	560	1,300	450	28	140	700
			03/04/11	17	620	620	1,100	42	420	2,500
			04/01/11	9.1	53,000	53,000	640	45	220	18,000
			05/06/11	6.6	3,700	3,700	420	16	81	1,300
			06/15/11	4.4	2,500	430	290	22	650	650
			07/01/11	1.6	900	59	100	12	20	270
			09/02/11	4.2	47,000	47,000	190	21	51	920
25	01115200	Shippee Brook	10/15/10	6.4	170,000	38,000	230	31	160	630
			04/15/11	8.6	3,200	1,900	240	42	240	1,100
			07/15/11	0.15	83	83	6.2	0.36	350	58
26	01115185	Windsor Brook	10/15/10	9.7	260,000	57,000	240	24	5.2	1,200
			01/21/11	14	520	520	360	35	81	8,000
			04/15/11	13	150,000	7,400	710	32	280	250
			07/15/11	0.21	120	120	12	0.52	1,100	81

Table 4. Daily loads of bacteria, chloride, nitrite, nitrate, and orthophosphate by tributary reservoir subbasin in the Scituate Reservoir drainage area, Rhode Island, October 1, 2010, through September 30, 2011.—Continued

[Water-quality data are from samples collected and analyzed by Providence Water Supply Board (PWSB); USGS, U.S. Geological Survey; ft³/s, cubic feet per second; CFUx10⁶/d; millions of colony forming units per day; *E. coli*, *Escherichia coli*; kg/d, kilograms per day; N, nitrogen; P, phosphorus; <, less than; >, greater than; shaded areas indicate values that were calculated with concentration data censored at half the detection level; alternate station names given in parenthesis for stations where different historical names were used for the same sampling location by Providence Water Supply Board]

PWSB station number	USGS station number	Station name	Date	Daily mean streamflow (ft³/s)	Total coliform bacteria (CFUx10⁶/d)	*E. Coli* (CFUx10⁶/d)	Chloride (kg/d)	Nitrite (g/d as N)	Nitrate (g/d as N)	Orthophosphate (g/d as P)
28	01115265	Barden Reservoir (Hemlock Brook)	10/12/10	3.3	190,000	12,000	210	48	88	7,300
			11/09/10	23	>620,000	>1,400,000	1,100	110	220	18,000
			12/14/10	94	>5,500,000	2,500,000	3,800	920	3,700	1,200
			01/11/11	7.2	4,100	700	230	18	120	440
			02/15/11	18	9,200	660	950	44	130	240,000
			03/08/11	200	340,000	84,000	5,500	370	320	1,500
			04/12/11	0	5,600	370	640	24	210	2,200
			05/10/11	11	12,000	12,000	790	27	100	12,000
			06/14/11	26	>1,500,000	290,000	1,000	250	3,500	3,500
			07/12/11	8.4	230,000	230,000	520	100	910	1,000
			08/09/11	8.5	>500,000	>500,000	310	83	910	6,700
			09/13/11	16	430,000	430,000	740	160	930	2,500
35	01115187	Ponaganset River	10/29/10	9.3	2,000	910	230	68	490	13,000
			11/05/10	37	2,200,000	140,000	1,800	360	680	4,600
			12/03/10	38	430,000	430,000	2,000	190	440	2,000
			01/07/11	20	11,000	11,000	920	49	310	9,600
			03/04/11	56	2,100	2,100	2,800	140	510	160,000
			04/01/11	36	20,000	20,000	1,500	88	50	3,700
			05/06/11	25	920	920	1,400	61	3.9	3,600
			06/15/11	21	12,000	12,000	1,500	100	220	1,000
			07/01/11	4.1	900	150	81	30	17	70
			08/05/11	0.32	3,600	3,600	5.9	0.78	19	3,500
			09/02/11	18	200,000	200,000	730	88	92	170

Table 4. Daily loads of bacteria, chloride, nitrite, nitrate, and orthophosphate by tributary reservoir subbasin in the Scituate Reservoir drainage area, Rhode Island, October 1, 2010, through September 30, 2011.—Continued

[Water-quality data are from samples collected and analyzed by Providence Water Supply Board (PWSB); USGS, U.S. Geological Survey; ft³/s, cubic feet per second; CFU×10⁶/d; millions of colony forming units per day; E. coli, Escherichia coli; kg/d, kilograms per day; g/d, grams per day; N, nitrogen; P, phosphorus; <, less than; >, greater than; shaded areas indicate values that were calculated with concentration data censored at half the detection level; alternate station names given in parenthesis for stations where different historical names were used for the same sampling location by Providence Water Supply Board]

PWSB station number	USGS station number	Station name	Date	Daily mean streamflow (ft³/s)	Total coliform bacteria (CFU×10⁶/d)	E. Coli (CFU×10⁶/d)	Chloride (kg/d)	Nitrite (g/d as N)	Nitrate (g/d as N)	Orthophosphate (g/d as P)
				Direct Runoff Subbasin						
1	01115180	Brandy Brook	10/05/10	1.4	800	800	7.3	3.5	72	300
			11/16/10	1.5	1,600	110	65	3.8	160	1,300
			12/16/10	3.8	14,000	100,000	85	28	79	720
			01/04/11	2.9	6,700	6,700	87	22	140	1,300
			03/01/11	6.5	24,000	1,400	280	32	12	1,400
			04/05/11	3.2	19,000	1,800	96	16	10	700
			05/03/11	2.8	17,000	1,500	84	7.0	0.43	190
			06/07/11	0.96	1,800	35	31	9.4	28	140
			07/05/11	0.42	240	15	6.6	3.1	45	5.2
			08/02/11	0.04	210	1.3	0.71	<0.01	16	610
			09/16/11	2.3	26,000	26,000	73	11	140	450
3	01115280	Cork Brook	10/07/10	3.7	>100,000	>220,000	43	18	78	190
			11/04/10	1.3	>35,000	>76,000	7.6	3.2	75	2,000
			12/02/10	5.7	>330,000	>330,000	72	42	150	200
			01/06/11	1.6	94,000	5,900	130	3.9	56	75
			03/03/11	6.1	>360,000	>360,000	600	15	54	2,600
			04/13/11	12	>700,000	70,000	940	88	13	280
			05/15/11	2.3	62,000	8,400	170	5.6	0.49	54
			06/02/11	1.1	>65,000	620	76	2.7	13	120
			07/07/11	0.18	2,000	170	11	1.3	110	0.24
			08/04/11	0.02	>1,200	11	2.1	<0.01	5.1	350
			09/01/11	1.1	>65,000	>65,000	89	5.4	57	480

Table 4. Daily loads of bacteria, chloride, nitrite, nitrate, and orthophosphate by tributary reservoir subbasin in the Scituate Reservoir drainage area, Rhode Island, October 1, 2010, through September 30, 2011.—Continued

[Water-quality data are from samples collected and analyzed by Providence Water Supply Board (PWSB); USGS, U.S. Geological Survey; ft³/s, cubic feet per second; CFU×10⁶/d; millions of colony forming units per day; *E. coli, Escherichia coli;* kg/d, kilograms per day; g/d, grams per day; N, nitrogen; P, phosphorus; <, less than; >, greater than; shaded areas indicate values that were calculated with concentration data censored at half the detection level; alternate station names given in parenthesis for stations where different historical names were used for the same sampling location by Providence Water Supply Board]

PWSB station number	USGS station number	Station name	Date	Daily mean streamflow (ft³/s)	Total coliform bacteria (CFU×10⁶/d)	*E. Coli* (CFU×10⁶/d)	Chloride (kg/d)	Nitrite (g/d as N)	Nitrate (g/d as N)	Orthophosphate (g/d as P)
4	01115400	Kent Brook	10/05/10	0.46	850	850	15	1.1	44	61
			11/16/10	0.42	15	15	3.8	1.0	110	170
			12/16/10	2.3	14,000	14,000	19	11	110	220
			01/04/11	1.8	180	66	25	4.4	19	210
			02/08/11	8.7	850	320	130	43	22	440
			03/01/11	9.1	53,000	330	220	44	1.1	160
			04/05/11	1.6	900	900	20	7.8	0.50	110
			05/03/11	0.9	500	33	11	2.2	11	20
			06/07/11	0.09	52	3.4	1.5	0.23	13	6.0
			07/05/11	0.04	1,100	23	0.72	0.20	130	260
			09/06/11	0.9	5,300	5,300	12	2.2	20	40
5	01115184	Spruce Brook	10/19/10	0.27	150	150	12	0.66	22	640
			04/19/11	5.2	2,900	2,900	200	25	300	92
			07/19/11	0.47	2,800	490	36	2.3	430	470
6	01115183	Quonapaug Brook	10/05/10	1.6	>43,000	>94,000	86	3.9	81	750
			11/16/10	1.8	1,900	1,900	200	4.4	320	1,500
			12/16/10	6.2	70,000	70,000	450	30	240	970
			01/04/11	4.4	4,600	1,600	380	22	310	160
			02/08/11	6.6	1,800	3,700	66	32	11	1,900
			03/01/11	13	48,000	24,000	1,200	32	3.7	490
			04/05/11	5.0	5,300	5,300	470	24	33	1,000
			05/03/11	4.2	4,400	4,400	390	10	120	250
			06/07/11	0.94	340	34	100	14	55	100
			07/05/11	0.3	3,400	3,400	5.0	9.5	130	730
			09/06/11	2.7	>160,000	>160,000	310	13	150	2,000

Table 4. Daily loads of bacteria, chloride, nitrite, nitrate, and orthophosphate by tributary reservoir subbasin in the Scituate Reservoir drainage area, Rhode Island, October 1, 2010, through September 30, 2011.—Continued

[Water-quality data are from samples collected and analyzed by Providence Water Supply Board (PWSB); USGS, U.S. Geological Survey; ft³/s, cubic feet per second; CFUx10⁶/d; millions of colony forming units per day; *E. coli, Escherichia coli*; kg/d, kilograms per day; g/d, grams per day; N, nitrogen; P, phosphorus; <, less than; >, greater than; shaded areas indicate values that were calculated with concentration data censored at half the detection level; alternate station names given in parenthesis for stations where different historical names were used for the same sampling location by Providence Water Supply Board]

PWSB station number	USGS station number	Station name	Date	Daily mean streamflow (ft³/s)	Total coliform bacteria (CFU×10⁶/d)	E. Coli (CFU×10⁶/d)	Chloride (kg/d)	Nitrite (g/d as N)	Nitrate (g/d as N)	Orthophosphate (g/d as P)
7	01115297	Wilbur Hollow Brook	10/07/10	<0.01	>270,000	>590,000	360	73	210	1,200
			11/04/10	4.5	4,700	4,700	160	11	200	270
			12/02/10	11	>650,000	>650,000	450	81	78	1,200
			01/06/11	6.1	600	600	590	30	210	3,700
			03/03/11	17	1,000,000	3,700	930	42	5.5	1,200
			04/07/11	8.2	4,600	4,600	250	40	81	940
			05/15/11	6.4	>170,000	33,000	170	47	56	310
			06/02/11	4.2	>250,000	2,400	330	10	270	180
			07/07/11	0.45	1,000	250	24	3.3	370	1,900
			09/01/11	6.6	>390,000	>390,000	130	48	120	390
8	01115276	Westconnaug Brook	10/08/10	2.3	2,200	2,200	55	5.6	99	810
			12/17/10	11	6,200	6,200	270	27	430	3,300
			03/11/11	15	1,500	550	510	37	68	2,800
			04/08/11	9.7	360	360	310	24	34	590
			05/13/11	8.1	1,800	300	390	20	420	4,500
			06/10/11	8.8	5,000	5,000	410	43	12	820
			07/08/11	5.6	3,200	3,200	390	14	390	550
			08/12/11	2.8	1,600	1,600	180	6.8	240	14,000
			09/09/11	17	620	620	820	42	25	72
9	01115275	Bear Tree Brook	10/19/10	0.49	1,100	110	26	2.4	9.2	390
			04/19/11	2.3	1,300	230	260	11	160	26
32	01115178	Unnamed Tributary 1 to Scituate Reservoir (Pine Swamp Brook)	10/20/10	0.18	100	100	4.0	0.87	40	300
			01/20/11	1.1	12,000	1,200	40	2.7	1.0	220
			04/21/11	1.0	570	98	38	2.5	930	9.2

Table 4.   Daily loads of bacteria, chloride, nitrite, nitrate, and orthophosphate by tributary reservoir subbasin in the Scituate Reservoir drainage area, Rhode Island, October 1, 2010, through September 30, 2011.—Continued

[Water-quality data are from samples collected and analyzed by Providence Water Supply Board (PWSB); USGS, U.S. Geological Survey; ft³/s, cubic feet per second; CFUx10⁶/d; millions of colony forming units per day; *E. coli, Escherichia coli*; kg/d, kilograms per day; g/d, grams per day; N, nitrogen; P, phosphorus; <, less than; >, greater than; shaded areas indicate values that were calculated with concentration data censored at half the detection level; alternate station names given in parenthesis for stations where different historical names were used for the same sampling location by Providence Water Supply Board]

PWSB station number	USGS station number	Station name	Date	Daily mean streamflow (ft³/s)	Total coliform bacteria (CFUx10⁶/d)	*E. Coli* (CFUx10⁶/d)	Chloride (kg/d)	Nitrite (g/d as N)	Nitrate (g/d as N)	Orthophosphate (g/d as P)
33	01115182	Unnamed Tributary 3 to Scituate Reservoir (Hall's Estate Brook)	10/27/10	0.13	1,400	120	4.1	0.31	61	59
			01/31/11	0.8	29	29	36	2.0	44	93
			04/27/11	0.54	300	20	27	2.6	300	2.4
			07/27/11	0.02	>1,100	110	1.0	0.0	1,000	49
		Moswansicut Reservoir Subbasin								
19	01115170	Moswansicut Reservoir (Moswansicut Stream North, Moswansicut Pond)	10/14/10	2.0	200	200	170	4.9	340	430
			11/15/10	2.5	>67000	>150000	210	6.1	49	260
			12/09/10	1.8	110,000	6,600	140	4.4	42	300
			02/10/11	6.2	230	230	530	30	37	1,000
			03/10/11	21	3,600	770	1,100	100	590	11,000
			04/14/11	14	1,400	510	1,300	68	61	1,200
			05/12/11	4.0	150	150	350	9.8	280	170
			06/09/11	3.4	7,700	1,200	260	8.3	0.82	290
			07/14/11	3.0	1,700	1,700	220	7.3	13	2,300
			08/16/11	12	22,000	22,000	770	29	590	980
			09/16/11	5.0	2,800	490	260	12	150	280
21	01115165	Unnamed Tributary 2 to Moswansicut Reservoir (Brook from Kimball Reservoir)	04/18/11	2.3	61,000	2,400	170	11	640	4.9
			07/18/11	0.03	120	12	0.68	0.33	3,100	220

Table 4. Daily loads of bacteria, chloride, nitrite, nitrate, and orthophosphate by tributary reservoir subbasin in the Scituate Reservoir drainage area, Rhode Island, October 1, 2010, through September 30, 2011.—Continued

[Water-quality data are from samples collected and analyzed by Providence Water Supply Board (PWSB); USGS, U.S. Geological Survey; ft³/s, cubic feet per second; CFU×10⁶/d; millions of colony forming units per day; *E. coli*, *Escherichia coli*; kg/d, kilograms per day; g/d, grams per day; N, nitrogen; P, phosphorus; <, less than; >, greater than; shaded areas indicate values that were calculated with concentration data censored at half the detection level; alternate station names given in parenthesis for stations where different historical names were used for the same sampling location by Providence Water Supply Board]

PWSB station number	USGS station number	Station name	Date	Daily mean streamflow (ft³/s)	Total coliform bacteria (CFU×10⁶/d)	E. Coli (CFU×10⁶/d)	Chloride (kg/d)	Nitrite (g/d as N)	Nitrate (g/d as N)	Orthophos- phate (g/d as P)
					Regulating Reservoir Subbasin					
14	01115110	Huntinghouse Brook	10/04/10	1.1	4,000	40	30	2.7	160	2,900
			11/18/10	24	25,000	25,000	480	120	120	1,200
			12/06/10	6.0	22,000	14,000	120	15	150	6,400
			01/03/11	26	150,000	150,000	600	64	2,800	62,000
			03/07/11	300	>14,800,000	460,000	4,300	1800	57	2,900
			04/04/11	13	12,000	1,300	380	32	16	1,600
			05/02/11	9.5	10,000	10,000	280	46	4,500	310
			06/06/11	2.1	24,000	7,700	210	10	120	15,000
			08/15/11	29	>1,700,000	>1,700,000	170	350	390	110
			09/15/11	4.7	>280,000	17,000	33	34	3,600	320
15	01115115	Rush Brook	10/04/10	1.3	4,800	730	140	3.2	120	1,000
			11/18/10	14	26,000	1,700	700	100	77	840
			12/06/10	4.9	>290,000	1,800	420	12	81	2,700
			01/03/11	16	9,000	9,000	820	39	1.0	32,000
			03/07/11	100	540,000	860,000	6,800	1100	2,500	1,200
			04/04/11	9.8	10,000	2,600	1,100	24	48	1,100
			05/02/11	6.3	37,000	6,600	650	31	44	220
			06/06/11	1.1	400	1,000	140	5.4	1,200	22
			07/25/11	0.04	230	230	4.7	<0.01	120	17,000
			08/15/11	52	>3,100,000	>3,100,000	2,300	1700	880	290
			09/15/11	3.9	100,000	23,000	120	29	7,900	350

Table 4. Daily loads of bacteria, chloride, nitrite, nitrate, and orthophosphate by tributary reservoir subbasin in the Scituate Reservoir drainage area, Rhode Island, October 1, 2010, through September 30, 2011.—Continued

[Water-quality data are from samples collected and analyzed by Providence Water Supply Board (PWSB); USGS, U.S. Geological Survey; ft³/s, cubic feet per second; CFU×10⁶/d; millions of colony forming units per day; *E. coli*, *Escherichia coli*; kg/d, kilograms per day; g/d, grams per day; N, nitrogen; P, phosphorus; <, less than; >, greater than; shaded areas indicate values that were calculated with concentration data censored at half the detection level; alternate station names given in parenthesis for stations where different historical names were used for the same sampling location by Providence Water Supply Board]

PWSB station number	USGS station number	Station name	Date	Daily mean streamflow (ft³/s)	Total coliform bacteria (CFU×10⁶/d)	*E. Coli* (CFU×10⁶/d)	Chloride (kg/d)	Nitrite (g/d as N)	Nitrate (g/d as N)	Orthophosphate (g/d as P)
16	01115098	Peeptoad Brook (Harrisdale Brook)	10/04/10	3.6	3,800	350	240	8.8	290	7,300
			11/18/10	50	26,000	26,000	3,800	370	54	720
			12/06/10	4.9	18,000	130,000	410	12	15	2,600
			01/03/11	18	33,000	33,000	1,500	44	8.3	2,000
			03/07/11	200	>9,500,000	>9,500,000	11,000	1200	640	2,600
			04/04/11	12	6,800	1,200	1,000	29	57	540
			05/02/11	4.4	50,000	4,200	570	22	42	88
			06/06/11	1.2	680	680	130	5.9	11	220
			07/25/11	0.68	1,200	1,200	86	1.7	47	1,900
			08/15/11	13	350,000	350,000	1,000	380	120	110
			09/15/11	4.7	8,600	1,300	250	11	29	290
18	01115120	Unnamed Tributary to Regulating Reservoir (Unnamed Brook A)	04/18/11	1.7	>100,000	1,800	180	8.3	260	11
			Westconnaug Reservoir Subbasin							
10	01115274	Westconnaug Brook	10/12/10	0.44	1,600	150	21	1.1	23	560
			11/09/10	3.8	22,000	22,000	200	19	23	970
			12/14/10	10	18,000	18,000	580	24	22	270
			01/11/11	1.2	71,000	120	100	2.9	4.0	2,300
			03/08/11	11	6,000	390	500	52	88	47
			04/12/11	1.9	1,100	70	140	4.7	290	320
			05/10/11	1.9	68	68	130	4.5	1.6	790
			06/14/11	1.8	>110,000	>110,000	95	4.4	15	48
			07/12/11	0.33	1,900	1,900	18	0.80	10	480
			09/13/11	1.8	1,000	1,000	97	18	14	37

Table 4. Daily loads of bacteria, chloride, nitrite, nitrate, and orthophosphate by tributary reservoir subbasin in the Scituate Reservoir drainage area, Rhode Island, October 1, 2010, through September 30, 2011.—Continued

[Water-quality data are from samples collected and analyzed by Providence Water Supply Board (PWSB); USGS, U.S. Geological Survey; ft³/s, cubic feet per second; CFU×10⁶/d; millions of colony forming units per day; *E. coli*, *Escherichia coli*; kg/d, kilograms per day; g/d, grams per day; N, nitrogen; P, phosphorus; <, less than; >, greater than; shaded areas indicate values that were calculated with concentration data censored at half the detection level; alternate station names given in parenthesis for stations where different historical names were used for the same sampling location by Providence Water Supply Board]

PWSB station number	USGS station number	Station name	Date	Daily mean streamflow (ft³/s)	Total coliform bacteria (CFU×10⁶/d)	E. Coli (CFU×10⁶/d)	Chloride (kg/d)	Nitrite (g/d as N)	Nitrate (g/d as N)	Orthophosphate (g/d as P)
11	01115273	Unnamed Tributary to Westconnaug Reservoir (Unnamed Brook South of Westconnaug Reservoir)	10/26/10	0.25	140	140	8.2	4.4	83	48
			04/26/11	2.0	1,100	1,100	240	9.6	14	820